The DNA of Pioneer Ministry

The DNA of Pioneer Ministry

Andy Milne
with Michael Moynagh

scm press

Published in 2016 by SCM Press
Editorial office
3rd Floor, Invicta House,
108–114 Golden Lane,
London EC1Y 0TG, UK

SCM Press is an imprint of Hymns Ancient & Modern Ltd
(a registered charity)
13A Hellesdon Park Road, Norwich,
Norfolk NR6 5DR, UK

www.scmpress.co.uk

Hymns Ancient & Modern® is a registered trademark of
Hymns Ancient and Modern Ltd

British Library Cataloguing in Publication data

A catalogue record for this book is available
from the British Library

978 0 334 05409 2

Typeset by Manila Typesetting Company
Printed and bound by
CPI Group (UK) Ltd, Croydon

Contents

Foreword
by Canon Mark Russell

Sitting on a wall in a housing estate on the north east side of Bradford, a teenage boy told me about how he had been on drugs, was regularly drunk, and how had his life not changed he was headed for prison. Today his life has been transformed and he follows Jesus. He said, 'Sorted saved my life because Sorted led me to God.'

One of the greatest privileges of my job as Chief Executive of Church Army is visiting our Centres of Mission across the UK and Ireland and hearing stories like this. God has used Sorted to change the lives of hundreds of young people, helped them break out of patterns of antisocial behaviour and set them on a different path following Jesus and becoming more like him. Church Army is so proud of Andy and Tracy Milne and their amazing work with Sorted. There are three congregations in Bradford, and now another Church Army Evangelist has taken the DNA from Sorted and is growing a fledgling youth congregation in South East London.

We can look to Sorted and admire all that has happened, but it is tempting to think that we couldn't possibly do anything like this because we aren't like Andy and Tracy, or we haven't been to Bible College or been ordained. This book says loud and clear, yes you can! God can use you!

I encouraged Andy to write this book because I wanted him to share the story of how Sorted grew, the things that went well, and the things that didn't go as well; to share his learning and wisdom.

My Church Army colleague George Lings' research into fresh expressions of church shows that if we want to reach the unchurched, and particularly unchurched young people, then it is projects like Sorted, pioneering fresh expressions, that are the best way to do so.

I pray that as you read this amazing book you will be inspired not just to thank God for Sorted, but that you will be inspired to have a go yourself! Could God be calling you to plant a new youth congregation in your area? Young people need to know God loves them, and young people need caring adults who are prepared to show them just how much.

I pray the legacy of this great book is that loads of new fresh expressions are planted to serve young people and help them follow Jesus in their lives.

Canon Mark Russell
CEO Church Army and Youth lead
on Archbishops' Task Group for Evangelism

Foreword
by Canon Phil Potter

Pioneers like Andy Milne remind me of the artist, L. S. Lowry. Initially working in obscurity, he painted Salford landscapes with the eye of a local and the heart of a northerner. The extent of his passion and skill were long hidden and sometimes ridiculed, but in time his paintings came to be classified as masterpieces. The shaping and pioneering of new forms of Church has a similar story – happening in secret, often unrecognized, painted by locals but celebrated over time.

The story of Sorted is an excellent example of this. Andy, too, worked from humble beginnings, living with and loving the locals, totally and naturally at home in his Bradford context with a bible and a skateboard. Over a decade later, not only has Sorted grown and reproduced itself twice, but the DNA of the pioneer has spread beyond his own community as similar fresh expressions have been planted in Thamesmead, London, and as far away as Nairobi in Kenya. Those are just two examples of projects that are directly linked to Sorted, but Andy's influence has been quietly spreading in all directions, inspiring many others to make a start in offering their skills and a missional heart for God to shape and use.

The clue to such an inspiring story is in the title of the book. This is not just another pioneer story, but rather a book that is laced with principles of good practice. Those principles may be simple and accessible, but this is by no means a 'paint-by-numbers' kit. Take the principles seriously, and Andy is offering genuine pioneers an authentic experience, one that will be fashioned by the Holy Spirit and will eventually bear much fruit.

I have a Lowry print called 'Group of children' hanging on my wall. It is beautifully simple and childlike, but powerfully evocative and unique. The pictures Andy paints in these pages are the same. They are painted by a humble man who offered his skills in a very ordinary setting, but I think you will agree as you read and enjoy this book that the results are extraordinary.

Phil Potter
Archbishops' Missioner and
Team Leader of Fresh Expressions

Acknowledgements

Thanks to Tracy, my wonderful wife, for your love and patience as we've followed this calling together, and to Sam, for being an amazing son to us. To Mum and Dad for always being there for me. To Emma and Patrick. To Alan and Mollie and to all in our wider family. Big thanks to Trevor and Lynn, also to Errol and Mavis, David and Pauline and Shirley, who helped me discover God and get going with him all those years ago.

To James, Laura, Samuel, Becky, Carl, Lynzi, Nick, Evelyn, Joshua, Gabriel, Damien, Simon, Val, David, Beka, Will, Anne, Michelle, Carole, Marva, Sharon, Ian, Ruth, Kathyrn, Robert, Lynn, Richard, Debbie, Kate, Sue, Tina and so many others who've helped make Sorted work. To all the many young people past and present – it's a privilege and a joy to know you and journey with you. To mention some of you by name is to miss others; you all know who you are – thanks!

Thanks to Mike Moynagh for advising me, helping to structure this book and reading over the draft. Thanks to David, Mary and everyone at SCM Press. To Karen Carter and Elspeth McGann for finding stories for the book. To George Lings, Andrew Wooding and Christine Gore for encouraging me to write.

Thanks to Stuart Hacking and Immanuel. Thanks to everyone at Church Army, especially Andrew Smith, Neville Willerton, Mark Russell, Des Scott and Richard Cooke. Thanks also to Steve Hollinghurst, Paul Deo and Ian Maher. Thanks to the old

Bradford diocese and the new Leeds diocese, especially David Lee, +David, +Toby, +Nick. Thanks to several local vicars whose help over the years has been essential for me and Sorted. Finally, thanks to numerous Christians from local churches who have worked with us, giving their time and support.

Introduction – the story of Sorted

While attending Bible college, I sensed a calling to get alongside young people and pioneer a fresh expression of church among them. By late 2003, my wife Tracy and I moved back to North Bradford with our newborn son, Sam, ready to begin.

The vast majority of young people in the Greengates, Idle and Thorpe Edge areas of Bradford had little or no church background. The area included two tough council estates with big social issues. Some parts of the estates are inside the top 1% of deprivation in the UK. The local secondary school was about to go into special measures, with many excluded young people, and the local councillors had recently compiled a list of young people who regularly caused mayhem and were a public nuisance. Welcome to my world!

There were lots of questions to keep me awake at night, but the biggest was. How do you begin to form church among young people in this area? It felt like our job was to build a house on a bog, with bricks that weren't shaped quite right and no cement! God help us – and he did.

We spent lots of time simply hanging out with young people in schools, on the streets and in the parks, looking for people of peace. We would often listen to their problems and stories over a game of football or while sitting on skateboards. Slowly they began to trust us. We began experimenting by forming little groups and asking ourselves the questions – How does the good news of Jesus connect with the lives of these young people? What might church look like for these young people if we begin it afresh?

Groups were formed in homes, playgrounds and porta-cabins through a mix of fun and friendship as a new Christian community began to take shape very slowly. Our work began with loving and serving young people, doing life together and addressing their needs by discussing both life issues and the good news of Jesus in ways that were designed to be relevant to them.

One learning curve was the discovery that the good news to these young people was partly met through our relationships and by becoming family together. How we accepted, treated and trusted them over the long haul was really important. This paved the way for them to listen to and believe our message and come to know Jesus themselves.

A eureka moment was the realization that we needed to work *with* the young people in everything to form a community. Many young people who didn't get along because they were in opposing gangs eventually came to accept, encourage and support one another in this new Sorted family.

A weekly pattern eventually took shape. We met for a big activity session each Friday evening, then for mid-week small groups, and finally a weekly worship service. Young people chose which bits they wanted to attend. Many began with the Friday session, learning to serve their peers in teams and hear a testimony that invited them to ponder whether God is real and what difference he makes. Some would then move on to question and explore faith at a deeper level through involvement in small groups. Others would then push further still by plunging into a life of faith and discipleship as they began meeting to worship and discover how God can start to transform their lives.

Sorted meets weekly as a series of 'stages', and young people can attend one, two or all of these different stages depending on their level of relationship with God. Most begin with one stage such as the Friday session, and then add other stages as they grow in faith.

After those first few years, Sorted went on to reproduce as God spoke clearly to us that this was to be our calling. Sorted 2 began in 2009 in the Bolton, Eccleshill and Wrose areas of

Bradford, with young people mainly from Hanson Academy. Sorted 3 began in Greengates, Idle and Thorpe Edge, with young people mainly from Immanuel College (the school Sorted originally grew out of). Sorted Plus+ is a Christian community of young adults, and Thrive is a Christian community of young families. Young people coming into Sorted as teenagers progress into Sorted Plus+ or Thrive as they reach adulthood.

Bantu Moses came to us on a Church Army gap year and returned to Kenya to begin Urban Hope ministries (Sorted Kenya) using the DNA of Sorted. Tracy Milne also took the Sorted model into a local Anglican church, applied the lessons we've learnt and saw significant growth. Nick Lebey spent four years as a Church Army trainee with Sorted and then moved to South London to pioneer a youth church called TYM (Transforming Youth Mission), using the Sorted DNA.

Sorted has sought to build relationships of acceptance and love, working with those we reach to develop Christian community together. Empowerment and ownership are vital components. We aim to be open to the Holy Spirit and true to God's word while travelling this journey as lightly as possible.

Sorted is a charity and a company limited by guarantee. We are a Church Army project and part of Church of England Diocese of Leeds as a fresh expression of church with a Bishop's Mission Order.

PART I

Early days – foundations

I

Beginnings – who are you?

A common problem in starting the pioneering process is working out where to begin. There might be many needs in your area suggesting several pioneering possibilities. Your church might have a list of hopes or expectations for doing mission. The pioneer might feel multi-gifted or simply unsure where to start. All this can lead to too many choices! So where does a pioneer begin?

September 2000

'What do you want to do when you finish college?' asked Tracy. I paused for a moment and thought hard.

'I'm not sure yet, I just want to do whatever God wants me to do,' came my non-descript answer, though it was an honest answer. I really didn't have a clue why God seemed to want me at college and what he had in store for me (if anything) when I had done the course.

'Yeah, but what really excites you, Andy? What would you really like to do when you've finished college?' Tracy kept on at me with her line of questioning. I suddenly remembered two conversations from the previous week. Both were about pioneering churches. Suddenly, without really knowing what I was going to say, I said it! One sentence that could be reduced to two fairly small words – two words that were about to change our lives!

'The thing that would really excite me is to start a church for young people – a church that is relevant, fun and God-centred.'

The sentence could of course be reduced to those two words 'youth church'.

Strangely, no sooner had I spoken this sentence, I sensed the Holy Spirit's presence. This sense of God's presence stayed with me throughout the next half an hour as we stayed on the phone chatting about what this could mean. As we chatted, a whole load of memories came flooding into my mind of youth work experiences, experiences of evangelism, people I'd talked to, books I'd read and teaching I'd heard; all these things seemed to have a theme running through them and that theme was 'youth church'.

'Can God really be saying "youth church"?' I asked Tracy as we neared the end of our conversation. We then spent some time giving our thoughts, feelings and future back to God, asking him to confirm this very sudden and unexpected sense of call to pioneer a 'youth church'.

Over the next few weeks, a whole load of things started to make sense, the feeling of being called to pioneer a youth church didn't go away and I had the chance to visit and study several examples of 'church among young people' in the UK scene at that time. I wrote a paper on what I saw on my travels and what I thought would be the way ahead. But the most important thing was to look back on my journey with God and see how he had been at work preparing me for this strange pioneering thing called 'youth church'.

Looking back – God the dating agency

During the late 1990s, Tracy and I went from being youth work volunteers together, to being prayer partners together, to becoming supportive friends for each other, until eventually we became a couple and decided to get married. With gifts and personalities that complement, Tracy and I being together would prove vital when starting Sorted. It would seem that God knew what he was doing years before we did (there's a whole story of God's guidance that there isn't space to share here).

Looking back – fun times in Leeds

As a young Christian, I found myself involved in evangelism, often among young people.

One Saturday afternoon while skating outside Leeds Uni, two brothers started to laugh and take the micky out of me because of a small 'Jesus saves' sticker on my skateboard.

'Are you some kind of Bible basher?' asked the younger lad.

'No, but I do believe in God,' I replied.

'You must be a bit dumb to believe in that stuff,' came the next attack.

'Well, I've seen God answer prayers to heal people, and people can even feel God near them when they pray. I can try and pray for you if you like?' I asked, trying to switch from defence to attack.

The older lad looked a bit surprised and paused for a moment.

'Er, yeah, OK. What do I have to do?' he asked.

We all sat down on skateboards (me, the two brothers, plus their two friends) and I explained a bit about who God is and then prayed over them all. Something powerful happened. I could see the lads really engaging with God. The next thing that happened was the two brothers both recognized that God had answered the prayer and had felt his peace.

The brothers apologized for the way they had teased me earlier and we started to get on really well. We chatted a lot about God because they were suddenly really interested and wanted to know more.

Two weeks later, after getting to know three more skaters in Leeds, I travelled to meet them and their mates in their home village of Yeadon. After skating for half an hour, the opportunity came to talk about God to one of the lads. Within a few minutes, everyone crowded round to listen. What amazed me most was how quiet and attentive the whole group of 15 were as I talked for about a quarter of an hour. God's presence was tangible in the playground, bringing such a peaceful atmosphere.

This led to many of these young people getting a touch from the Holy Spirit after prayer with the laying on of hands. Shortly afterwards, four lads were completely healed from wrist and ankle injuries they had picked up through skateboarding. All the young people and I were totally amazed at the power God showed as he instantly healed these guys.

I would always follow up these experiences by explaining how to become a Christian, sometimes leading them into a prayer of asking God to come into their lives and then encouraging them to become part of a local church. It was this last part that usually went wrong. Let me explain.

Looking back – it's over here, or is it?

The two brothers mentioned above did try visiting a local church but found it boring and didn't understand any of it. I tried to invite loads of skaters to a youth Alpha course in my local church but it was unrealistic to expect them to travel by bus at night to my part of town because, even though God was now cool to them, it didn't mean they associated finding more of God with going to church (as you or I might do).

I also met weekly with a different group of skaters to pray and read the Bible in my parents' house. They sometimes came to my church, so we did youth Alpha with them and the church youth group, which went fairly well, and later took them all to Spring Harvest. But although the church was warm and welcoming, it still felt like someone else's world to them. They would say things like, 'They are nice people but . . .', or the comment I heard repeatedly was, 'Why don't we just keep meeting at your house, Andy, to do the Bible study for an hour, and then go skating afterwards?' They wanted Jesus, but didn't feel at home in the local church.

Over a few years, I saw lots of young people come to faith in Jesus but never felt comfortable in an existing church. This is something that troubled me for years, but I could only start to see a solution when God called us to set up a youth church.

Perhaps planting a church within their culture would provide a solution to the problem I had been experiencing.

To summarize, God calling us to pioneer a youth church was the third part of a triangle of reflection from God. The first part had been Tracy and I coming together; the second part had been the early mission experiences I had in the mid to late 1990s among mainly non-churched young people, which taught me some lessons but also left me with many questions.

Lesson – beginning the pioneering process starts with prayer, discernment and reflection on our journey with God

The apostle Paul, perhaps the Church's greatest pioneer, tells the church in Ephesus that God has a plan for their lives and he is working in them to fulfil his purposes (Ephesians 1.11). It's the same for us today. If God wants you to pioneer something then he will already have been at work in your life preparing you for the task ahead.

But how do I find out what God wants me to pioneer? If we start by praying, discerning and reflecting on our spiritual journey then some of our questions about pioneering (e.g. Am I called to pioneer? If yes – where/when/how?) may start to be answered. So how can we do this practically?

1 Praying and seeing what God is doing

Good ideas are OK, but God ideas produce spiritual fruit and a harvest. There may be good ideas for mission in your church, or lots of needy situations that shout out, 'Come and pioneer over here', but we should really seek to know what God is wanting us to do. In fact, all Christian ministry can be described as seeing what God is doing, then joining in!

'I pray that the eyes of your heart may be enlightened in order that you may know the hope to which he has called you ...' (Ephesians 1.18). Paul writes to the Ephesian Christians, praying that they see the hope God has for them. This was a church that pioneer-planted several other churches in Asia Minor, and so clearly part of God's plan for these Christians was that they would reproduce several times. We might expect Paul to give loads of practical advice on how to pioneer success-fully, but instead he starts by asking them to pray and see. We too should ask God to help us see what he is doing in us and in our situation.

As we go through the following steps, it is good to do each step prayerfully so that through the process we might see more clearly.

2 *Looking back*

Often we have to take a look back at our journey with God so that we can make sense of what God is calling us to do now. His story in our lives will inform our future with him. There are lots of practical aids that can help us to look back reflectively.

One practical aid is to write or map out a timeline of your spiritual journey so far, highlighting key moments and time periods on the way. Do you ever write a journal? If so, you may want to read through journal entries over a period of time. Other people might prefer to create, draw or paint to help them reflect. Still others might value sitting down with a person they trust and simply telling the story of their journey while asking the other person to prayerfully listen. There are no right or wrong ways to look back, it's about which aids work for you. Don't rush one of these exercises, take a couple of hours or do it over a few days so that you can really reflect deeply.

Whatever aid you use to look back, it's good to ask ques-tions, such as:

- What areas of work have I tended to serve God in?
- Is there a pattern of how I've been serving that is emerging?
- Are there particular people groups I've worked with most?
- What are my gifts? How might God use my gifts in pioneering?

The answers to these questions are designed to help us spot emerging patterns which God may have been working through to prepare us for a pioneering task. For example, my reflections pointed me towards pioneering with non-churched teens, but your reflections might point you towards young families or young adults or something else.

3 Can you reimagine yourself as a pioneer?

In the early years of Sorted I was given the labels 'detached worker', 'schools worker' or 'local churches worker' as people saw an aspect of what I was doing in the early stages of the pioneering process. In some ways, this became a test of whether I yielded myself to one of these labels, choosing to settle permanently into one of these roles or persevering with God in his calling to pioneer a youth church.

Often, changing the way we view ourselves is the hardest change to make as it can mean seeing ourselves in a totally new light. We may have to reimagine ourselves as pioneers of a new thing that doesn't yet exist. This is tough because some people will find it hard to believe the thing is ever going to happen until it actually arrives. Pray that God helps you to imagine yourself in the role he's calling you to, and that you will be able to overcome doubt when others fail to see.

4 Does the pioneering idea fulfil a need?

When I took the idea of 'youth church' to people in two different areas, it was obvious that there was a need for that kind of thing. In other words, a culture gap existed between the local churches and local young people; there were hardly any young people in those churches and a new C of E secondary school provided an opportunity. If there had been thriving Christian youth work in the area, then it might have been the wrong place to start.

Do you have a pioneering idea? If so, is there a need for your idea to work in helping people become part of a new church? If you don't have an idea yet, what are the local needs? You could get a small group of friends to pray about these needs to try and discern if God wants you to start serving these needs as the start of a pioneering process.

5 Are there pioneer role models doing similar things?

Role models can inspire us with confidence in pioneering. As I prepared to start Sorted, Mike Breen's pioneering work at St Thomas Crookes was an inspiration to me.[1] At college, my tutor George Lings[2] inspired me to read Acts with a church-planting lens and think differently about new ways of doing church. Role models can inspire, be an example, provide insights and teaching on pioneering and forming church that can be very supportive and foundational as we go into new territory to work out how to pioneer something new. Who are your role models? Do they inspire or inform your pioneering? Your role models may be a good reminder of your pioneering roots, not to be copied but to be inspired and informed by.

6 Where do you begin?

While pioneers have often been sent long distances to begin work, in the post-Christian UK context we are starting to appreciate that God often uses us to pioneer where we are. Tracy and I found ourselves moving back to Bradford to start Sorted in an area where we had lived. Without really planning it this way, we knew the culture of the area and understood much about its people; we knew the local church, and some of our very first volunteers were Tracy's friends – these were all big advantages to begin with.

What have you got that God might want to use? It could be familiarity and knowledge of a local area and its people. It could be expertise in a business or line of work that gives you an 'in' to that subculture and its people. Don't discount what God has already given you. Local pioneers are needed in so many local contexts where the Church has lost ground or within new people groups and subcultures where the Church has never had ground.

7 Getting help from others

This whole process is often made easier when we involve others. From close friends to prayer partners to local ministers, we can ask them to pray and discern with us, involving them in the whole process of looking back and reflecting on what God has been doing in our lives. We might also want to involve a spiritual director or someone with similar expertise in helping to discern how God is at work in a person's life. There is likely to be someone from your diocesan office, churches network office, a Fresh Expressions network office or someone known by a local minister who can help.

When assessing if there's a need to pioneer locally or when wondering where to begin, it's important to involve others from the outset. Other local Christians should help to clarify whether the vision should be implemented in the local context. Finding discerning but open-minded people is key. If a local permission-giver such as the local minister is discerning but not enthusiastic about pioneering, you will need to carefully choose the appropriate time to speak to them. The vision will need to be credible, and so some discerning and clear thinking might need to be done before a conversation happens. However, if discernment leads to serious planning, the local permission-giver might feel things are running ahead without his or her involvement and this could breed mistrust or tension.

Thirst – by Sue Butler in Romsey Town, Cambridge[3]

'Thirst has grown out of 11 years of relationship and prayer. As parents of primary school children, we used to meet outside the classroom at "pick up" time.

One parent, Rachel, wanted to pray about something and, out of that meeting, came an idea for a monthly prayer breakfast. That group formed the basis 11 years later for Thirst. As we began to pray for the school, other people started coming to faith and getting healed and saw answers to prayer in their families.

Things began to move in a different direction in my own life. My children were getting ready to leave the primary school for secondary school, so my personal involvement there might naturally have ended. My husband started ordination training at Ridley. I began to increasingly feel that God was saying that my time and connection with the school was not over but that there was more that God wanted me to do there.

My husband's Ridley friends kept asking me why I was not at Ridley training for ministry as well! At that time, I'd reply that there was no chance that I had been called to be a vicar. Somehow God was combining my relationships, family life and calling to a place where he has already been at work. Like Moses, I felt that God asked me to take what was in my hand and use it in a wider setting.

I was talking to God about it and told him, "It's no wonder people don't go to church." I "heard" the question, "What would they come to then?" I thought of what we did as friends together: breakfast, drink coffee, pray together, laugh together, have relationship and support each other. I said to my friends, "Let's keep on drinking coffee but, if it's going to be church, it has to have more to it than a coffee morning. It's about transforming the community that we live in through our relationships, and in the power of the Holy Spirit."

We didn't begin straight away because I was too apprehensive of starting something that did not last once it became official. So, we prayed about it for about a year before we started meeting in the school lounge in November 2006. We served good coffee, food, fruit and juice. Everybody invited friends and we had about 30 people there at our first gathering.'

Sue remembered that, during the years before Thirst, a discerning gifts course revealed to her that her main gift was pioneering. She was inspired by stories of missionaries in Sunday school books, her missionary parents and Christian pioneers such as Gerald Coates. By looking back on her spiritual journey, listening to the needs of the community and prayerfully seeing what God is doing, Sue was able to begin the pioneering process that led to Thirst.

Notes

1 Paddy Mallon, *Calling a City Back to God*, Eastbourne: Kingsway, 2003.
2 George Lings – see www.encountersontheedge.org.uk.
3 Story by Sue Butler, at https://www.freshexpressions.uk/search/node/thirst.

2

How do I form a team?

Tracy, Sam and I moved back to Bradford after several years of being away. We had come back with a sense of calling to pioneer a youth church. How would we start? What would we do? Most importantly, what did God want us to do?

I knew that getting a good team together would be crucial. A team would enable us to do things that we could never resource on our own; it would bring together people with different gifts and give us the chance to form a mini community that would become the foundation of a new church.

A pioneer without a team has more chance of failing. There are many things that you just can't do on your own. Jesus had the disciples and Paul had Barnabas, Silas and Timothy. Finding a team should be at the top of a pioneer's priority list.

Finding a team

Back in Bradford we were initially linked to three local churches that were to supply us with about ten adult volunteers. We knew we would need a team big enough both to work with young people and to share the burden of all the practical jobs that would be happening behind the scenes. This would be needed to make a youth church function well.

Unfortunately, volunteers were not exactly jumping out of the churches to help us. We recruited only four volunteers from these local churches. Many were willing to pray but few were willing to get involved – isn't this often the case? We quickly realized that we needed God to help us if we weren't going to fall at the first hurdle!

Tracy picked up the phone and asked two couples (not from our supporting churches) to help us out. For two months, I visited and invited several people to become volunteers with Sorted. We then started meeting to worship, pray and discuss the vision of youth church planting with the small team we were assembling. By January 2004, we had gathered about seven adults including Tracy and me. One of the couples would become an important foundation stone in Sorted over the next few years.

Every Friday night we would meet together in the hall of a local primary school. I would prayerfully choose one key plan, value or topic that would be crucial for us to get our heads around before we really got going with the youth work.

Several things were happening as we met together for the next six months. Relationships within the team were slowly form-ing, strengthening and gaining momentum. These relationships would act as the glue to hold us together through both the good and tough times that lay ahead. Team members were get-ting a chance to find out whether this whole thing was for them (two left before we even got started), some were emerging as key members and we all spent time soaking in God's presence as he prepared us for the work he had called us to.

Forming a team wasn't without its problems. We lost people because they didn't really buy into the vision or values. Others simply couldn't cope with some of the young people we were called to get alongside. By the end of the training period, we really weren't sure if we had enough team members or if we had the right ones. This raises a problem for all pioneers – how do you know what the right size of team is for your work? How do you know you've got the right team members?

What size should your team be?

Ultimately, only God knows what the size of your team should be. The pioneer project and how you do it will be influenced by the number of team members God gives you. After praying and trying everything to recruit the right people, you may find that your plans need adjusting if you find you have more or fewer volunteers than you expected.

When we started Sorted 1, we began the work with seven adults including Tracy and me, which was just about enough, but a couple more would have really helped things. When Sorted 2 got going, there were ten and then eleven at one point. We certainly didn't need eleven in the first couple of years but as some volunteers dropped off, it made life easier because we didn't need to search desperately for replacements. So what factors will influence the size of team you aim to find?

Context

Big youth sessions will need lots of DBS-checked adults. Groups for older people will also need several adults to help out. Groups for young families might only need a very small team if new parents from within the group can help, but this isn't always possible. Groups for young adults might only need a small team if the young adults are involved in running the group themselves, but if the group contains many vulnerable young adults, there will need to be trained team members who are DBS checked. Context also influences how quickly some of the new people can become part of your team. For example, younger teens can play an important role, but legally they can't carry the responsibility of adults. Parents within a group for new families might provide new team members fairly quickly, so the initial pioneering team can afford to be small. Certainly, the sooner a pioneer can find new team members from within the context, the easier it will be for the team to adapt its approach to the needs of the context.

Numbers

The number of team members can determine the number of new people you are able to work with. However, it's always possible to add new team members as the number of people you work with increases. The best way to do this is to develop indigenous team members from among the new people you are reaching, adding them to the original team when they are ready.

Prayer and recruitment

I have often had the problem of not enough team members and rarely had the problem of too many. In Luke 10, Jesus said that the harvest will be plentiful but the workers few in number, so we should ask the Lord of the harvest to send workers. Pray for the right team members to be found and plan carefully how you might recruit. For many pioneer initiatives, it's likely that the first place to start is by sharing your vision with local churches. As you share your pioneering vision or idea, it is likely that some people will want to get involved – although don't be put off if no one does, just try the next church on your list or visit again in six months' time.

During the first two years of Sorted, I had to make it a priority to share the vision with churches on Sundays, visit church leaders in their homes and visit individual Christians. I would simply look for people who love God, love people and are humble enough to want to come and learn together as we start to pioneer.

What about 'not yet' Christians joining the team? We've had some great 'not yet' Christians on team, but make sure they are respectful of our faith and view it in a positive light. The majority of your team do need to be Christians so they can engage in prayer and be witnesses to the new people.

Have you got the right team?

Probably not! Jesus didn't have the right team but it didn't stop him from getting started and using that team to begin the worldwide Church. Jesus' team included Judas the traitor, Peter who denied involvement with the team when the going got tough, and James and John who were glory-seekers.

So perhaps the questions should be – Is the team right enough? What safeguards should be in place? How can we train and develop team members?

Sorted's criteria are simple. Does the person have a heart for people and are they willing to learn? Is the person honest, trustworthy and reliable? And, in the case of Sorted, are they suitable and safe to work with young people?

CCPAS (Churches Child Protection Advisory Service[1]) suggests interviewing potential team members to check suitability, asking for two character references, giving a three-month trial period, and getting DBS checks (if the volunteer has contact with children, young people and/or vulnerable adults). They have excellent guidelines for recruiting team members, as do many local volunteer agencies. Please check them out to find out more about safeguarding checks. The rest of this chapter will focus on how to train, develop and form a team for pioneering churches.

Forming a team is a process

Jesus took his team away from the crowds to rest and be refreshed. During these times he taught his team in more depth than he taught the crowds. Time to teach, rest, pray, do life and journey together were key parts of Jesus' strategy as he developed his team. Many of his team would go on to pioneer churches across the ancient world. What can we learn from these principles?

Teach

Different people, brought together with little or no experience of pioneering, all with different life experiences and different identities, will take time to mould into a new team with its own identity. With Sorted 1, I planned six weeks of training sessions but this became six months! Why? As we prayed and thought about team development, it didn't seem right to stop the training. I now think six months is much closer to what is needed.

Relationships of trust and dependency don't magically appear overnight. Vision and values don't become shared overnight.

This doesn't mean that the team has to wait six months before doing any pioneering; a little pioneering might enhance the learning by providing experiences to reflect on. But be careful the pioneering work doesn't snowball before the team has gone through its formation period, otherwise the team might die in the avalanche.

Each Sorted training session started with space for coffee and a chat, letting people unwind and catch up after a busy week. In Sorted 2, team members would then take turns to bring a couple of songs on CD for the worship time. Giving team members the opportunity to take turns in doing refreshments, CD worship and leading prayers at the end of the session gave us the chance to practise operating as a team in a safe space before the pioneering really got going.

After worship, we would take one value or important lesson and spend an hour doing a training session, with teaching from the front, space for discussion and interactive learning exercises. These training sessions were the main way the team came to share the same values and vision. We explored topics such as how to relate to young people, listening to what God is doing in the mission context, empowerment, teamwork, listening and encouragement, Jesus' mission methods, and church planting in the Bible.

One big learning curve is to learn to enable new people to discover God as participants and enable new people to take ownership within the developing church. In other words, we don't provide mission/service/church, but we enable and facilitate. This is the only way a church will become incarnated within the local culture. We all needed extra time to learn this concept and unlearn being providers. Putting this learning into practice was a long process, as was learning to enable and facilitate, but it was worth the wait when it happened.

Prayer

If God starts mission and our role is to join in, then our pioneering work will be more fruitful if we can find out what God is doing. Prayer is the main way our spiritual eyes

(Ephesians 1.17–18) are opened to see what God is doing. When we pray in teams, it's important to give space for people to pray, listen and discern. Some team members may receive words and pictures, others may discern wisely or just get the sense the group is on the right track. It's good to give space to encounter God, asking him to give each team member what she or he needs for the task ahead. We would always spend a few minutes praying after each training session.

Social

People live busy lives and your team might say they are too busy to meet socially. We had to be creative in carving out social times so that we could do life together, have fun and get to know each other a bit more. One idea was to meet monthly for a prayer breakfast before Sunday church. We figured that everyone eats breakfast, especially the kids; and so meeting at each others' houses for a bacon sandwich, a good chat and a short prayer time with the kids was just the trick. As well as building vital trust, social time makes you more than just a team, it kick-starts you into becoming a small Christian community or family. New people will spot the deeper relationships of a Christian family and find this attractive.

Journey together

Every person beginning with a pioneering team is starting a journey. Mike Moynagh shows how a team member's identity will go through a process of change as they become part of a team.[2] Each person is likely to start with an identity consisting of who they are at work and home but also who they are as a Christian within their local church. When they join a team, they may imagine and explore several possible identities of who they are within this new community that is forming. Finally, after quite a while they are likely to have formed a new identity that incorporates who they have become within the new church. Some people will have to travel much further than others because the new community will be so different from their previous experiences. These people are likely to need more support.

The pioneer can't travel this journey for the individual team members but he or she can travel alongside and be supportive. Two of our team sacrificed their summer holiday for several years to take young people to the Soul Survivor festival. One person initially worked with the young people but sensed a call to work with young parents; another switched from youth work to becoming treasurer. The pioneer should try to be aware of the journey facing each team member and do whatever they can to be supportive. Exploring different possible roles with people, and allowing people to try something but switch roles later on, is one way to support. Encouraging and affirming everyone's contribution and listening to individuals throughout their journey is important too.

Many pioneers will be so mission focused that they easily miss these long-term journeys. If that could be you, is there someone in your team who could be that supportive person? You may need to empower that person to be the main support to the others in the team, but you will need to listen regularly to the supportive person. You will also still need to do some of the supporting, otherwise some in your team might mistake your mission focus for a lack of care.

Progress report

After three years with Jesus, the disciples doubted, denied Jesus and didn't fully understand his mission. What should we expect from a team after six months of training? It's realistic to expect some to doubt, most will have ongoing questions and one or two might drop off because it's not for them. It's OK to lose a couple of people, just as it is OK to gain a couple of new people along the way. Paul parted with Barnabas, but the mission continued. However, it's important to have a core of people who have been through the training together and have come to a point where they share the same vision and values.

Some team members will be more passionate and involved than others, different gifts will emerge and others will become loyal servants. These differences are likely to be enhanced as the team starts the pioneering work. Some will struggle and take time to adapt, while others will flourish.

Keeping the team together

We were fortunate to have held on to approximately half of our volunteers as the first five-year mark passed for each Sorted. This may seem a short or long time to you. The context and place we are called to pioneer in will influence the length of time, as will an individual's circumstances, yet we can all put ongoing things in place that will lengthen the average time that an individual stays in the team.

Regular team meetings

When working among tough, street-wise yet vulnerable young people, sometimes a team member's role is to serve sacrificially. Some of our team members have struggled to relate to the young people, yet their role in serving and supporting has been vital. I've discovered at our monthly meetings that starting with a vision report to highlight good news stories really encourages the team, while prayerfully planning the way ahead gives a sense of God's purpose and confidence that we know where we are heading. Space to listen to team members and take on board their comments is also vital.

Conflict is sure to arise. Creating an environment of regular team meetings, prayer, training, social time and rest will help to reduce conflict as trust, communication and dependence on God are built into the team experience. But when conflict does occur, taking time to really listen and empathize with people's concerns may reduce conflict, as will clear communication. The leader needs to get involved and try to resolve the conflict, but while he or she should try and alleviate conflict, it's important to stay focused on the vision and not be dragged off course.

Prayer

The pioneering starts with seeing what God is doing and joining in. We should keep this focus as we pray, while also bringing before God the needs of individual team members and those we are serving as we meet.

Training

As the pioneering gets going, loads of new issues and learning opportunities will arise as the team start running groups and meeting new people. Once in a while, it's good to do some training to address the issues and enable learning. If your team has a monthly team meeting then making it a training session twice a year could be one solution.

Social

Keeping a light and fun atmosphere within the team will help the team deal with issues and disappointments while strengthening the relationships. Having a social once in a while will help this to happen. How does your team prefer to socialize? Is it over a pint in the pub, dining in a restaurant, or something completely different?

Rest

Confession time – I've not always got this one right, but I'm working on it. I now know how important it is to make sure team members take time out when they need it and don't do too much. Remember to love them and their families.

'Community worship' – led by Caroline Hakkinen (rural Leicestershire)[3]

In 2007, Caroline Hakkinen saw that something else was needed to reach people in her village because the two existing Book of Common Prayer church services were a bit alien to most folk. With the absence of a vicar, Caroline as churchwarden felt it was right to bring together a few people to discuss the problem. Some wanted a traditional church service, yet others wanted a new child-friendly service geared for the needs of non-churchgoers. Eventually, consensus was found and the focus was for something new, fresh and inclusive that would listen to local people and base the service around their needs.

Shortly afterwards, a few people became a team that put together 'community worship'. They would share all the roles of praying, reading, talks, hymns etc. between the team. There was no outright leader to call the shots, instead Caroline acted as co-ordinator and an emphasis was placed on listening to each other, sharing the tasks and using their gifts together. Seven years later, 'community worship' continues to be a fruitful fresh expression of church led by a team of lay people, with a visiting priest sitting in the congregation from time to time rather than leading it.

They will regularly invite people from outside the team to participate. Help was given to these new members if needed. The team itself would meet regularly to review each new service; care was taken not to criticize individuals themselves but instead to recognize things that weren't working and find new solutions.

Teamwork has been one key to the success and sustainability of 'community worship'. The same idea has been tried twice elsewhere, but Caroline reckons it didn't work as well because the churches focused the idea on a person as leader not a team. Teamwork, sharing the task, listening to each team member and reviewing progress together are key components at community worship.

Notes

1 www.ccpas.co.uk.
2 Michael Moynagh, 2012, *Church for Every Context*, London: SCM Press, 2012, ch. 12.
3 The story about teamwork at 'Community worship' is from an interview with Carol Hakkinen.

3

Where do I find support, and how can we create good, sustainable partnerships?

A short story

A few years ago, Sue started pioneering with good support from her local church. They knew Sue was gifted in evangelism and so they wanted to support her while they all hoped that a new church would develop within two or three years.

As time went by, Sue made lots of contacts with new people and built good relationships. Many of these new people were struggling young parents and so Sue started a group to chat about parenting skills. The group was well attended and led to the formation of a second group to discuss spirituality. Over a couple of years, lots of people attended these groups; some were moving closer to God and two adults were baptized. Most of those moving closer to God were attending Sue's groups, while others were known to Sue through the local community. There was a real sense that God was doing something, but Sue wasn't sure how it would develop and become church.

By now, people in the supporting church were expecting to see a new congregation emerging. 'Two new adults baptized are OK,' they said, 'but will this work ever come to anything?' Sue the pioneer was troubled by their comments. Secretly she asked herself the same question. Sue's local minister was acting as her mentor. When meeting up with him, she would ask his advice about how to develop the work so that it would eventually become church. The local minister was very supportive, but would often look a little blank when Sue brought up this question. He had been very enthusiastic at the beginning, but nowadays his enthusiasm wasn't so obvious. After a while the local minister would avoid the question as he clearly had no idea what to do. Sue soon found it difficult to get a meeting with him; his diary was always full, unlike a couple of years earlier. Sue started to worry and wonder where a solution to her problem would come from. She was feeling increasingly isolated and no one around her seemed to have any idea of what she should do.

Following a random conversation at a conference for pioneers and fresh expressions, Sue got connected with another pioneer called Jo, who lived about 20 miles away in a nearby town. Sue started meeting with Jo once a month over coffee to chat about Sue's problems. Jo had been involved in pioneering work for a few years and had some helpful suggestions, giving Sue food for thought. Jo advised Sue to invite someone to visit her and her local minister to talk about the long-term plans for the new fresh expression that was emerging. The local minister seemed relieved by the idea of meeting someone whose job was to visit pioneering initiatives and offer support and advice. He showed enthusiasm for the first time in months. So a meeting was arranged for Sue, Jo, the local minister, two key local church members and a consultant (with expertise in pioneering) to get together.

Both Sue and her minister were full of high hopes as the meeting got under way. The minister was impressed by the consultant's understanding of pioneering and ability to make sense of what God seemed to be doing through Sue and others. Jo was able to share real-life stories of how she had learnt to find solutions to pioneering problems within her context. Everything was going really well, and bringing together different people with different gifts to talk was certainly bringing support to Sue. After the meeting, Sue felt less isolated, her work had been given value and meaning; she went away feeling encouraged and hopeful. There would be other challenges ahead but at least now a supportive coalition was being established.

Not sure what the next step is? Feeling misunderstood or wondering whether what you are doing is on the right lines? We are not called to struggle and face the challenges of pioneering alone. Sometimes we might feel like Jesus in Gethsemane when he asked for prayer and support from Peter, James and John. Jesus was annoyed when the three disciples fell asleep instead of supporting him, so he knows how it feels to experience a lack of support.

Finding the right support

After pioneering several churches, being beaten and nearly losing his life once or twice, Paul never doubted that God would provide all that he needed, writing to the Philippians, 'my God will meet all your needs according to the riches of his glory in Christ Jesus' (Philippians 4.19). My experience as a pioneer has taught me that God does equip those he has called. It has not always been obvious where the support is but somehow it has always been there. I have usually had to pick up the phone or take time out to go and visit someone, be vulnerable and listen more than I would always like. However, through this process God has provided me with the right support from a variety of people.

Close friend or partner/spouse

I'm thankful to be married to someone who I can be myself with, say it as I see it, and still be valued and listened to. Tracy and I have been there for each other throughout our journey. Having someone we can turn to in the darkest moments and say honestly what's in our hearts, trusting that person to listen, value and accept us, is what makes a true friend. I think pioneers need at least one person who they can talk to from the bottom of their heart, whether it's a close friend or spouse.

Practical support

In the early days of pioneering Sorted, my local minister gave me great support in lots of ways, especially when it came to our practical needs as a family. For his kind support, I will be forever grateful. As Sorted got going, we were soon getting into unknown territory and neither he nor I had the relevant experience to address some of the issues arising.

Encouraging support

After a couple of years, some local leaders started to doubt whether this youth church would ever happen. Doubts quickly became contagious! Doubts about the project quickly became doubts about me as a pioneer. One or two questioned my approach and whether I had the gifts and ability to do the job. This was an extremely hard time. I felt the doubters were looking at the work from the wrong point of view, comparing our speed of development to the speed it would take to set up groups among those already connected to church. This is why they couldn't understand why it took so long.

Their contagious doubts then caused me to doubt. 'Why are things happening so slowly, God? Will it ever happen, God?' Several years on, I can now look back and see that all of us were on a big learning curve and we all came through it relatively unscathed, but at the time it knocked my confidence for almost two years. Despite all this, some of their doubts were healthy. They caused me to wrestle with things, taught me a lot, pushed me into experimenting more than I might have done otherwise and made me determined to make Sorted happen.

It was about this time that two guys I worked in partnership with became a great source of support. They believed in me and gave me encouragement as they saw good things happening with young people. They gave value to the incomplete, messy but fruitful pioneering work that was happening, both encouraging and offering advice and insight as to how to keep improving and developing things. This was just what I needed at the time. God was at work in the small networks that I was building, in individual lives, and his kingdom was breaking in. Pioneers need peers who can encourage and value the work they are doing, especially when it's undeveloped, incomplete and it isn't at all obvious it will become church.

Creative thinking support

During the days of doubt, I would visit a mentor who gave me support from another angle. He was full of ideas and insights of how to develop things so that we would get closer towards the goal of youth church. Some of his ideas were great, some I left alone and others got me thinking creatively and positively about situations where I had only previously seen obstacles. Pioneers need to think creatively all the time, finding solutions to new problems that crop up. Over a three-year period, this mentor helped me to see the glass half full and turn problems into opportunities.

Pastoral support

Another person provided much wisdom in tricky situations when I was trying to handle the doubters or tricky people. He was often a calm voice of reason, giving good advice when I needed to know how to keep people on my side, or at least not alienate them further. This calm voice of wisdom and pastoral support has been there in the background throughout Sorted.

Objective support

In recent years, I've learnt to travel once every six weeks away from Bradford to speak face to face with another mentor. Talking through stressful situations, complex problems, being asked where Jesus is in my life at that moment or gaining strategic insight has been really helpful. Finding someone who can provide objectivity and ask the hard questions provokes serious reflection. This mentor knows me pretty well and knows my work pretty well.

God has provided me with different people to support me at different times. I am really grateful to everyone who has supported me in one way or another. Looking back, I'm thankful to have had two or three people supporting me at any one time. Some people supported me for a short time, while others supported me for a few years. Different supporters have different gifts and strengths – some are pastoral, some understand the people you are working with, others have expertise in helping pioneers in a variety of contexts, and others understand how to work with local churches or your denomination. Sometimes it's been a case of choosing the right person for the right situation or ringing up two or even three different people to get a different take on the same problem. At other times, the supportive person has been a supervisor, and so the length of the person's role as a supporter is to some degree dependent on the role they are given. When this role has ended, they are still on the end of the phone as an advisor but can't get directly involved in an active way. As Proverbs 15.22 says, 'Plans fail for lack of counsel, but with many advisors they succeed.'

How to find the right support for you

1 Pray and ask God to help you find the right person or people

God knows exactly what kind of support you need. He wants to support you both by his Spirit the comforter and through others, so when you need support, don't forget to go to God first as well as talk to others. We should pray fervently so that we get the right support.

Once I was thinking about who to ask to be a mentor and thought about a well-known minister with gifts in mission work. Tracy prayed and sensed God wanted me to ask a different person because he would help me keep focused on character development. As she spoke, I sensed the peace of God, and the second person turned out to be the right support for me at this time.

2 Reflect on what kind of person you need at this moment in time

I find this hard to do alone. I would suggest involving others in helping you discern the kind of support or supportive person/people you need around you. People support in all sorts of ways – encouragement, problem-solving, pastoral care, creating ideas, listening, challenging and enabling you to work things out yourself. This last kind of support is perhaps the most important because we grow the most when we have to work things out.

3 Listen really well and be vulnerable

Pioneers need to lead their teams and take a lead much of the time, but when meeting a supportive person it's important to take off the leader hat and put on the listening hat. When we've shared our pains or problems, sometimes it's good to make ourselves vulnerable and listen to what is said. Of course we need to weigh up the advice and discern what is best, but only after carefully listening and pondering on it. Obviously, you can only make yourself vulnerable if you really trust the person supporting you and respect their advice and wisdom.

4 Get help to find support

Are you part of a network of churches (e.g. diocese, circuit or group) – is there someone within the network who can point you towards potential supporters?

5 Peer support

Find other people doing pioneer work or similar work. You might meet together to learn from each other and support each other. When we meet with others doing the same sort of work, we often learn new things, meet those facing similar problems, gain new perspectives on familiar challenges or hear stories that encourage us. Our peers probably need to hear our stories and find out how we overcame difficulties, so support works both ways.

6 Long term

Be open to some people supporting you for several years. Having people to journey with you over a period of time allows them to know you and your context better, trust is deepened, and their advice is probably even more helpful because it is likely to be more appropriate to you and your situation. The knowledge that a good long-term mentor has of you will give them greater understanding of your strengths and weaknesses. This means they are less likely to tell you how to suck eggs, but will sensitively challenge your weaknesses. A long-term mentor will have seen something of your journey over several years. My long-term mentor is someone I first met 17 years ago when he became my supervisor for a part-time course I was doing; he then became my personal tutor during my training, which ended 11 years ago. He has since been a mentor to me for the past six years!

7 Specific skills

There might be many specific new skills needed within your pioneering team, such as chairing a meeting, getting annual accounts audited, disciplining young people, safeguarding issues, policies for a whole range of things such as safeguarding/ volunteers/equal opportunities etc., fundraising, getting charity status, managing and recruiting volunteers, and so forth. My advice would be, first, to prioritize what specific skills are needed at that moment in time. For example, safeguarding was an important area we needed to learn about early on, but getting charity status didn't occur to us until a few years later.

Second – delegate! The pioneer leader's job is to make sure these skills are learnt and implemented by one or two people in the team when they are needed, but if the pioneer tries to learn to do everything then he or she runs the risk of being distracted from the main people engagement work which is likely to be their calling. The pioneer will probably have to learn some things, but God shares his gifts among the body and so a one-man or one-woman band is not an option.

Third, when you've prayerfully planned and decided which skills need to be learnt and who should learn them, make it a golden rule that for anything significant you do for the first time, from chairing meetings to raising money, you ask advice from someone who has done it well. And if you don't know someone who has done it well, keep asking others if they know someone, until you find the person!

CPAS Arrow

CPAS (Church Pastoral Aid Society) has been running the Arrow leadership programme[1] for a number of years. Having done the programme, it taught me a lot about support. Arrow takes groups of leaders from different denominations (pastors, trainee pastors, youth workers, children's workers, evangelists etc.) who are aged 25–40 and each head up teams of leaders (volunteers or paid staff).

Each Arrow programme lasts 18 months and over that period a support network is created for each member. I found myself in a peer group of four and we met together periodically to support and encourage one another. We would listen to each other's stories, encourage and offer advice sensitively, praying for each other before we left for home.

We were each assigned a learning mentor who met with us at each residential to discuss how our lives and ministries were progressing in relation to the three simple aims of Arrow (to be led more by Jesus, lead more like Jesus and lead more to Jesus), which cover our spiritual life, personal life, our close relationships and our work for God.

At the start of the course, we were asked to find a mentor whom we could meet every few weeks to discuss similar issues. I still meet my mentor to this day.

Phone a friend

Every contestant on the TV show *Who Wants to Be a Millionaire* has several people they can phone if they choose the 'phone a friend' option. Why? The contestants don't know what subject will come up so they need several people with knowledge in different subjects. Pioneers need several differently skilled people because we don't know what problems, issues or opportunities are coming our way.

Volunteers also need to be allowed to seek support from other suitable people as well as the pioneer. I found that, on some issues, volunteers would come to get support from me, while on other issues they would talk to Tracy. But good communication is needed between the various support people so that wires don't get crossed!

Partners – creating good and sustainable partnerships

While watching an old Indiana Jones film, I saw a scene where Indiana has to cross a huge chasm with an enormous drop. He is trying to reach his destination on the other side of the chasm where the Holy Grail is being kept in a cave. The only way across the chasm is to risk putting his foot down firmly on to the thin air of the chasm, while believing a stone ledge will suddenly appear and catch his footstep. The ledge will catch his foot and stop him falling to certain death. As he takes his first step of faith, a stone ledge appears just in time to catch him, and then other stones appear with each step he takes as he crosses the chasm. This makes it possible for Indiana to continue his journey and reach his destination on the other side.

In pioneering work, our God-given vision is the destination, and yet our journey is over a chasm of potential pitfalls. Partnerships can become the stone ledges needed to help us to cross the chasm and reach our destination. Without partners to provide people, use of buildings, finance and prayer support, much pioneering work is likely to fall into the chasm! Partners are often used by God to provide support and resources for fledging pioneering work.

Partnership meltdown

When we started Sorted, we were supported by several partners including one national and several local organizations.[2] I had a good relationship with one particular organization and felt respected and supported by them. There was trust and they gave me a lot of freedom to start Sorted in the way I thought it should happen.

As time went by, this supporting partner began to struggle financially and Sorted was asked to make a financial contribution towards it. Sorted had some money that had been donated by two couples, which was set aside specifically to pay for youth work resources. We were suddenly pressed by this partner to donate half of this money towards their struggling organization. In those days, we banked with this partner and relied on them in many other ways, so this made things complicated.

I explained to this partner that, while I sympathized with their financial struggles, Sorted would not give up money that was ring-fenced for youth work, especially when it was donated with that specific purpose in mind. Anyway, I was accused of being mean and my relationship with the leader became difficult. Reasonable communication became awkward for a while. I didn't know whether Sorted would survive or whether this partner would pull the plug and Sorted would go under. It was a really tough time. I was saddened because I had known the leader for years, but also felt the situation we were being put in was unfair.

A second partner came to the rescue. A representative from another organization met the leader and a solution was found. Sorted ended up paying half of the money initially asked for by the first partner. I didn't think Sorted should pay anything (neither did the mediating partner), but it was worth it just to ensure Sorted survived and to try and mend the relationship. We started banking elsewhere and things improved following this solution. In one sense, when the problem erupted, Sorted were extremely vulnerable, but we were helped out by the mediation of the second partner.

A while later, a new person took over leadership of the first partner organization. Our relationship with this organization was back on track, so things were now hopeful. As it turned out, the new leader liked Sorted but misunderstood our vision and therefore felt threatened. We found ourselves thrown back into conflict over a number of issues.

Once again, other partners mediated and tried to help, but things only calmed down when Sorted agreed to move away to share a building with another local organization. Sorted lost one-third of its young people in the process of moving elsewhere! It was the young people who paid a high price, although it was no fault of theirs. We survived both these conflicts with the same partner, but when one of those stone ledges is removed suddenly and unexpectedly, the chasm below can soon dance before your eyes.[3]

Creating a web of belief

Laura Dunham describes networks of partners in early stage pioneering ventures as 'webs of belief'.[4] These are built like a wall, one brick at a time, as the pioneer builds relationships of trust with several partners. This leads to the resourcing and support of the pioneering venture. Every pioneer needs a web of belief so that positive partners support the project in very practical ways in order that it becomes resourced.

Mike Moynagh writes that to create a web of belief, the pioneer and partners must develop shared goals, emotional identification, credibility, and the pioneer must sometimes be ready to go the second mile for the partner.[5]

How does a pioneer create and sustain a web of belief?

1 *Shared goals*

At the very start of the pioneering process for Sorted 2, I went to chat with several local vicars about my ideas. I sensed God wanted us to form a second youth church. I knew that it was vital that they caught the vision for a youth church so I tried to be as clear as possible. If partners don't share the same vision we soon have di-vision! Fortunately, the local ministers were pleased that it might happen in their area because all of their churches were struggling to connect with young people from the local secondary school.

It's important to have integrity and be clear about what your vision is and what it isn't, so that partners don't get false hopes of something that isn't going to happen. For example, I always say that our vision is not to get young people into the existing churches. If a few young people end up in those churches then that's great, but we're not going to promote this because our vision is to create church with the young people.

The vision really does need to be shared. Listening to your partner's ideas will provide wisdom that might help the mission, but will also assure the partners that we are all in this together. For example, a local partner might have better information about where a suitable building might be or which people might be good to invite on to the team. Certainly the local ministers knew the best local people to invite on to the Sorted 2 team.

2 Emotional identification

Forming good relationships and trust are key factors in helping partners develop emotional identification with the pioneering work. When Sorted started, it took patience and time to earn trust from some partners. I was new and unproven and so one partner was reluctant to give us too much freedom in school, but this changed as the relationship deepened and I became trusted. This is normal and understandable when a youth worker first goes into a school. The school came to appreciate the pastoral work I was doing with individual young people. My relationship with the school staff deepened until both they and I realized that we shared many of the same values, such as accepting young people and working with them just as they are.

I was initially invited to help out once a week at the school lunch club. My aim was to build relationships with lots of young people, so I knew that I needed to be in the school at least two or three times a week to achieve this. New opportunities came along at the school after a few months. These included assemblies and, most importantly, the chance to do some detached youth work at lunchtime on the playground.

The school had been reluctant to allow detached work, perhaps because there was more risk in allowing a youth worker to wander round the playground, even if the school could keep a watchful eye on me. At the time, I had been invited to go on a trip to Germany. I wasn't sure about this trip; it was a full week off the job at a time when the job really needed to get going. Then I heard that the head teacher of the school was going on the trip. Perhaps this would give me the chance to chat to her informally about doing the detached work. After praying and trying to listen to God, I decided to go on the trip. I did get the chance to speak to the head teacher over an evening meal and she did give me the thumbs up for the detached work!

Moynagh mentions the importance of social perception, social adaptability and good social skills.[6] This means treating your partners as people, who love, care, get hurt and have feelings that need attention. It means we have to build a warm relationship with our partners when possible, not just settle for a cold agreement. I've sometimes struggled to find time to do this properly because pioneering has taken most of my time, but it's important to work out what each partnership relationship requires and do what you can.

3 Credibility

In another situation, we mistakenly allowed young people we didn't know into a primary school we were renting. The young people started exploring the head teacher's office and were caught in the act by the caretaker! We got a deserved telling off because we hadn't thought to obtain permission from the school to allow young people into the building.

A year later, when we started renting a church to invite new young people into our session, we had learnt our lesson. We were very careful to seek permission, lock up rooms that were off limit, and take good care of the building. Inevitably when there are 40 young people at a session, something will get damaged now and again. From the first time we met, we decided to always phone the owners immediately and offer to pay for repairs when damage happened. While this is just common sense, the owners started to trust us and we have been renting that building for ten years because they know we will pick up the phone and take responsibility for our actions. Going the extra mile to be consistently honest, responsible and reliable will really help build relationships of trust. Partners respect you more if you are quick to own up to a mistake and say sorry rather than make excuses (but they also expect you to learn your lesson too).

Little actions increase credibility. For example, with supporting local churches, I've discovered that giving an update to the congregation is a great way to tell good news stories, to thank them for their support and to ask for help. As new people discover God through the pioneering work, a couple of brief testimonies are like gold dust! Sharing good news stories about the work, coupled with testimony and heartfelt thanks, will increase credibility in local churches. Some churches will want this fairly regularly (two or three times a year), while others just once a year.

4 Going the second mile

Over the years, I've found that schools work involves a partnership of give and take. For example, we sometimes help others to run lunch clubs even if detached work alone is the most fruitful choice for Sorted. If a lunch club becomes largely unfruitful for Sorted halfway through the school year, we will stick with it until the end of the school year because it supports the school's lunchtime provision of activities, it keeps young people happy and it demonstrates to the school that we are partners prepared to give, and not just take.

A 'give and take' approach builds trust in the long term. The church buildings we use all have an element of 'give and take'. At the time of writing, we pay rent to two churches and preach regularly in a church that has no minister and is always on the lookout for preachers. All these churches are generous partners to Sorted and yet it's important that we are giving something in return. Another supporting church has several PCC members who volunteer for Sorted. Their reward is direct involvement and knowing that God is working among young people of the local area.

Coalitions of partners

Bringing all your partners together for a meeting can be either good or bad depending on how supportive the most influential partners can be. When Sorted 2 got started, we were blessed with good partners and the most influential vicar of the group was very supportive. His support was pivotal. It made working with this coalition great fun and took away many worries as I never had to question whether these partners were supportive or not.

However, I've also experienced meetings of partners where it can work the other way. In one coalition, two key local partners were quite negative and would continually question everything. I was always fearful that their negativity would rub off on to the other partners and put doubts in their minds. When gathering a coalition of partners, it's vital that there are key people in the meeting who are not just supportive but bring wisdom, knowledge and experience. We've been blessed to have people with expertise in fresh expressions and young people/schools work present at our coalition meetings, and they have been invaluable to us down the years. As a pioneer, I would make every effort to remind these busy people of the date of the next meeting and encourage them to be there as their presence would make such a difference.

If you find yourself struggling with negative partners, you will have to weigh up whether it's best to invite them to the coalition meeting with the hope that they are won over or whether it's best to visit them one to one to try and build a relationship of trust for the time being. Of course, you might not get a choice of who to invite, which might mean it's even more important to meet up with a negative partner in between meetings, with the hope of establishing a relationship of trust.

The Melting Pot – by Jules Middleton[7]

'I found myself in the somewhat unenviable position of chairing a meeting of several local churches. It was the first time that all of them had agreed to meet with a common goal, and – coming from the only fresh expression of church in the area – I think I carried with me the awareness of other people's suspicion. My hope was that we could find a way to work together; a way of working built on the essential foundation of prayer. Let's face it; churches are notorious about not wanting to work together.

Moving forward from that initial meeting, I am delighted that we have managed to do this, having just celebrated the first birthday of "The Melting Pot" – a community café which the churches now run together. Our combined interest was to reach an area of a nearby village which had long been overlooked, sneered at and ignored, and it was about time we changed that.

Of course, running the café hasn't been completely plain sailing! Making relationships is key to the heart of any missional outreach, not only with those we are reaching but also with each other. We've needed to work within, and yet also stretch, each of our boundaries and barriers. As a fresh expression of church, we have a Bishop's Mission Order and are licensed to cover two deaneries, but that isn't to say we can then stomp all over other clergy's "patches". We recognized that careful conversations and planning behind the scenes would be the backbone of what we were aiming to achieve but in acknowledging that knowledge and desire, we knew that misunderstandings could still happen because — even within the same denomination — we sometimes speak different "languages"!

Another part of the learning curve is that we must be realistic; knowing that we are unlikely to be united in all things but being clear that the purpose of the project has to be something which we are most certainly in agreement about. There's no doubt that having complete clarity on this can help avoid challenging conversations later down the line.

Coming from a fresh expression of church, we had always assumed (admittedly with an unspoken hope) that this café would — in time — develop into its own fresh expression but how, and when, that happens was really up to God and our first priority was simply to make relationships and bless the area. However, I've subsequently learned that if the phrase "church plant" looms on the horizon, it can strike fear into many a church minister — however much well-intentioned planning goes on!

Like any relationship, a degree of compromise is required. We have had to learn to work together, pray together, and find a unity that we can focus on.

After 18 months, we are really only just developing those key relationships with each other and with local residents, so time will tell where and how the café develops but, for now, we are just taking it one step at a time. I really believe that the future of the Church as a whole relies on us uniting and reaching out: united in that love we share. Jesus' "new" command to love one another is just as relevant now as it was then: By this everyone will know that you are my disciples, if you love one another.'

Notes

1 CPAS Arrow Leadership Programme: www.cpas.org.uk.
2 See 'How can we get support?', Share booklet 04 by Mike Moynagh and Andy Freeman, at www.freshexpressions.org.uk /share/booklets04.
3 I have kept the descriptions of the partners mentioned in the story above deliberately vague to preserve anonymity.
4 Laura Dunham, in Michael Moynagh, *Church for Every Context*, London: SCM Press, 2012, p. 275.
5 Moynagh, *Church for Every Context*, p. 275.
6 Moynagh, *Church for Every Context*, p. 279.
7 Story by Jules Middleton at www.freshexpressions.org.uk/views /ecumenically-challenged.

PART 2

Getting started – beginning the pioneering work

4

How do you plan? Learning to think in stages

Here are a few common planning problems faced by pioneers:

1 'I won't copy someone else's model because we shouldn't clone church, but starting by looking at the context makes it hard to plan anything at all. People at my local church think I don't know what I'm doing because my plans sound too vague.'
2 'If I plan ahead then it all looks too fixed but when I look at the context to work out how to plan, it just looks confusing and messy. How do I plan in such a messy context where people's lives are chaotic?'
3 'I've tried doing an act of worship but the people here are just not ready for it. I've been getting alongside them and we have great relationships but I can't get them moving forward another stage in their spiritual journey.'
4 'I want to listen for God's guidance, not make my own plans!'

Caught in a trap?

Some pioneers feel caught in a trap. Most textbooks rightly tell us that we shouldn't copy someone else's model of church but should 'listen' to the context we are pioneering, adapting the new church to meet the needs of the people we are trying to reach. This leaves a question – How do I prayerfully plan ahead while being flexible to the context?

Rigid and inflexible planning could become a pioneer's blind spot, blinding him or her to seeing the needs or culture of the people and make the necessary adaptations for how a new church is formed. This might make it hard for new people to fully connect the gospel message to their lives because it is not being made relevant enough.

Alternatively, if we don't have a clear aim and some ideas of how to achieve that aim, there is a good chance that we might never get to where we want to be. If the vision is so vague that we don't know which direction to start walking towards, then we could end up anywhere! Is there a solution to these planning problems? One answer is to think in terms of 'stages of development'.

Starting out

During my first year in Bradford, we started hanging out informally with young people by playing football and doing skateboarding in the area where I lived. Despite a couple of young people finding God, we simply weren't going to meet enough young people this way to start a youth church.

After the team training was complete, the adult volunteers started to get alongside and chat to young people in the local area (doing detached youth work) in pairs. Although this gave them an insight into the culture of local young people, most found it very challenging and weren't cut out to approach complete strangers on a street corner or in a bus shelter, especially teenage strangers, and so this wasn't very fruitful.

A third attempt at mission happened as I started co-leading a lunchtime club in Immanuel College. We played fun games and did short talks, but it was hard to build deep enough relationships through this once-a-week club. As I prayed, I sensed that I needed to be in the school more often but in a different role.

In 2004, I started doing detached youth work on the playground of Immanuel. Over the next couple of years, I got to know loads of young people. Going into school to simply listen and get alongside young people was initially limited to one big group of skateboarders and their mates, as they were the most open to me being around. It took longer for many other groups to accept me, but over time contacts were made. These contacts led to the building of trust and the starting of friendships. I still know many of these young people today.

In April 2005, following conversations with some of these young people, we started our open youth session on Friday nights and simply invited young people from the playground and the neighbourhood. By the end of the summer, we had about 30 young people meeting to skateboard, play football, chat and listen to music.

We would do a short talk or discussion about God or a life issue halfway through the session. The young people had no church connection and so we were talking about God to a crowd that seemed uninterested and rowdy. Despite one or two young people coming to faith, it was a big achievement just to get the group to listen for five minutes each week! We kept asking – How could we get lots of these young people connecting to God and change this crowd into a Christian community?

Focusing on what mattered

We stumbled on the answer to the above question as we kept focusing on being relational. Over the next year, many of the youngsters from the Friday-night crowd would meet with Tracy and me or another couple during the week in small groups.

Some little groups prayed and read the Bible because they had a key young person who was open to doing that. Others just chatted, and we prayed for opportunities to share our faith as we opened up our home. As the next year rolled on, relationships deepened and quite a few young people started a journey of faith. Looking back, the community of adults that had met in 2004 was expanding and starting to become a community with the young people.

Late in 2006, we sensed God wanted us to start a worship service. How could we do this and stay true to our values of being both relational and giving young people ownership? We decided to ask key young people – those who were finding God in the small groups – to join with us in starting a worship service. We planned everything in detail with the young people because we wanted them to own it. So the conversation went like this: I said we needed a worship time, they said we needed a break in the middle of the service. I said we needed teaching from the Bible, they said it had to be fun and interactive. So together we worked it out and it challenged us to really listen to them and affirm what they contributed.

As the service got going, we found that the most important part of the service was experiential. We experimented with different ways of praying but discovered that many young people found God when we prayed and asked the Holy Spirit to come upon them. It was difficult to get young people with short attention spans to be still and quiet as we waited in God's presence, so we hit upon a way of praying that really works with them. We would pray and ask God to come by his Spirit. With their permission, we would pray specifically for two or three key young people with laying on of hands, before releasing them to go and do the same for their peers. We followed just behind!

Young people with short concentration spans were staying focused because they were participating and taking an active part in the process.

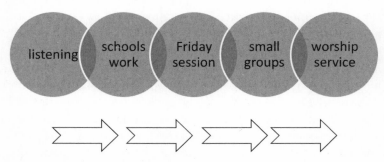

Figure 1: Stages of a spiritual journey

Without us ever planning it this way, we began to see that Sorted had distinct stages of a spiritual journey (Figure 1):

1 Listening to young people.
2 Schools work where relationships started.
3 An open activity session on Friday nights for young people to discover Sorted and hear a short message about God.
4 Small groups where they could ask questions and discuss faith, starting to become disciples.
5 Youth worship service to encounter God and go deeper with him.

All of the stages became crucial to its success: people with little or no previous church connection find it easier to progress through a set of stages than to jump straight into stage 5 – acts of worship like a service can seem alien at first. We found that relationships, ownership and faith in God often deepen as young people add another stage. This is partly because you meet them more often but also because each stage has a distinct purpose that builds on the previous stage.

Planting seeds of faith happens in both the school and the open session, but young people often find God and become Christians in the small groups and worship service. You might ask: why bother with the schools work and open session if the small groups and worship services are where young people find God? Relationships and trust need building in stages 2 and 3 so that the deeper teaching, prayer and worship happens in a safe environment – an environment where young people feel unpressured and able to discover God at a pace they are happy with.

If young people drop out of the worship service for a while, it's easier for them to come back because they are still part of Sorted on other nights. The young people already have a sense of belonging by the time they find God in stages 4 or 5, which means they are more likely to stay in Sorted and be nurtured and become disciples of Jesus.

Why stages?

We are increasingly living in a post-Christendom world in the Global North. Lots of people think church is like a tin of soup, but with a label that gives the impression the product inside isn't worth having. The small print on the label says things like 'Church is boring and irrelevant, judgemental (anti-gay people and anti-women) or simply not for them.' In other words, they think they know what Christianity is by the label on the tin. They don't know that the essence of what is inside the tin is truly priceless – a dynamic relationship with a God who loves us completely, giving us the fullness of life and a caring family! Although many people don't like the look of a tin of 'church', as pioneers we want to both show and tell them what is really inside the tin – this dynamic relationship with a loving God.

What does this mean for pioneering in the Global North? In most contexts, starting a new church by inviting people to worship is like trying to sell a tin of soup that no one wants. Although there are some places where this does work, in an increasing number of contexts we can't start with worship because people will only see us trying to sell a tin of 'church' and they think they know what's in the tin.

Mike Moynagh argues that birthing a church is a practice that encompasses a whole range of skills, just as playing football professionally is a practice.[1] Much has been written about birthing churches using a 'worship first' approach. This has provided a body of knowledge and expertise over many years but while this is still relevant in some of the USA, it is becoming increasingly irrelevant in much of the UK and Europe.

It's better to start by using a 'serving first' approach, getting alongside people and building relationships so that the first thing they see is Christians are OK because God's love works through us. In other words, we have to be the good news, earn respect and build trust so that in time they will be ready to hear and consider the good news. When this happens, they forget

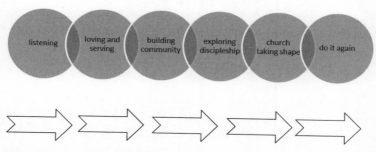

Figure 2: A 'serving first' journey

the label on the tin and start to be genuinely surprised by what is inside the tin. This is why it makes sense to use stages of development when pioneering a church.

Less is known about the 'serving first' approach as a practice and the literature is still in its infancy. Moynagh and Freeman have developed the model of six stages outlined in Figure 2, based on studies of churches using the 'serving first' approach.[2] This model is an adaptation of an earlier model by Croft, Dalpra and Lings.[3]

Stage 1 – listening

Listening can happen through a variety of ways: checking out any community research and questionnaires, community surveys and social reports into a geographical area, or cultural research through reading magazines and surfing the web to understand a particular subculture. All these things can be valuable and well worth doing, but in my opinion having conversations with people living in the area or network you are trying to reach is irreplaceable. Just listening to people's stories, hopes, aspirations and problems will give the pioneer vital insights into people's lives. Ask questions to find out the issues and needs that are big in people's lives. Talk to lots of people and try to have honest and open conversations where people feel they can open up to speak to you. It's often good to compare what is said in conversations with community research.

Listening can provide a cultural map from which you can start to creatively plan ways ahead.

Stage 2 – loving and serving

This stage is about building relationships of trust and respect with key people in the pioneering context. This might be done through serving people in a cafe where conversations happen or taking part in creative projects such as cleaning up an estate with local residents. Alternatively, it could be done through direct conversations during detached youth work, opening a counselling service or offering spiritual healing. What opportunities are there for you to get alongside and start having lots of conversations with different people?

Serving can help build trust and respect but ultimately it should be part of an ongoing conversation with the people we are reaching. Some churches simply build skate ramps and offer free drinks to young skateboarders. This is great but it's much more effective to have a chat with the local skaters and find out what kind of ramps they want rather than just assuming. If we then involve the skaters in buying the ramps or building them together, the ongoing conversation and joint project will automatically deepen the relationships and trust if we really listen to each other throughout the process. So serving works best if it's part of a conversation where the pioneer and new people listen to each other and work together.

In Luke 10, Jesus tells his followers to look for people of peace when they do mission. Mike Breen has described people of peace as 'people already prepared by God' as door openers and bridges to build connections with new people in the mission context.[4] Relationship-building should be done prayerfully with an eye open for people of peace.

Stage 3 – building community

When we've spent a good deal of time building relationships with new people, it is likely to be very messy, with unconnected individuals dotted about. It's good to explore prayerfully with your team how you might start to gather these individuals together so that a community can begin to form.

Be creative, think outside the box, share ideas and do all of this with some of the key new people you are building a relationship with. What kind of things will people want to come along to? What are the needs and interests of the new people? How might your idea build genuine community? It could involve meeting in a pub, cafe, workplace, leisure centre, community centre or church hall. It might take place around food, shared activities, creating a space for spiritual seekers, or something completely different.

If we're to pioneer new churches then it's important we find ways to sow seeds of faith when we gather new people together. What will work in your context? It might be sharing a short gospel message over a shared activity, such as 'Jesus is the bread of life' with a group baking bread. It might be providing a space for questions and discussion about spirituality and life. It might be creating space for people to draw, write or create something. Connections could be made with what is created and the Creator of the universe. Space to meditate, pray or practise spirituality might be relevant in some contexts. Some of the keys are:

- involve the new people in the planning so they start to share ownership
- offer the gospel, don't force it
- be ready to ditch something that doesn't work and try something else but also discern when to preserve.

Stage 4 – exploring discipleship

This stage started for Sorted because we wanted to take a smaller number from our big gathering and discuss faith in God using the Bible and praying together, just as Jesus preached to the gathered crowds and then went deeper with a smaller number of disciples.

The focus of this stage is about exploring faith, conversion and disciple-making. It's about creating space to discuss God with those who really want to know more. There are many ways to do this – what will work in your context? Are there key people ready for such a group?

Stage 5 – church taking shape

As we found ourselves with several tiny groups, we wanted to create a space for worship, deeper teaching and a place where people could encounter God through prayer in the power of the Holy Spirit.

Stage 6 – do it again

Having been through the stages of birthing a church once, you will have the knowledge and experience to do it again. Is God calling you to do it again? If so, pioneers can re-plant churches, as we read in the book of Acts. This will cause churches to be multiplied so that many more people can find a relationship with God.

We will explore how to make each of the six stages work in practice in Chapters 5 (stage 1), 6 (stages 2 and 3), 7 (stage 4), 8 (stage 5) and 10 (stage 6) (Figure 3). Each chapter will take one or more stages, then share stories and methods while exploring ways to meet the challenge of implementing each stage and overcoming potential hurdles.

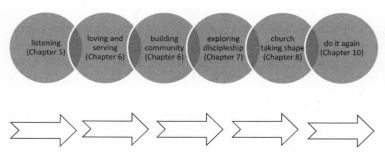

Figure 3: The six stages in practice

Greengates parish church, Bradford, late 2014

When my wife Tracy was asked to spend a year seeing if Greengates parish church could be turned around, it was both a challenge and an opportunity to put some of our learning from Sorted into a totally different context and see what would happen!

Having grown old together, the existing congregation consisted of 14 people, the vast majority being over the age of 75. The one glimmer of hope was the busy Jolly Tots mums 'n' toddlers group, run by the churchwarden each Monday afternoon.

Tracy and co set up a series of stages as they reach out to young families in the parish. Jolly Tots and the two monthly social nights (Ladies night and Family night) build community and bring together over a hundred people. Stepping Stones was then formed as the next stage of church, with young families meeting after school each Tuesday to dramatize interactive Bible stories and contemplate what these stories might mean for them. Discipleship is being explored at Stepping Stones and it's exciting to see.

After much prayer, the PCC decided that if the existing Sunday service was revamped to cater for young families, the culture gap between the traditional elderly congregation and the new young families would lead to a botched compromise pleasing no one. So the existing trad service continues each week at 9.30 am and at 10.30 Foot Steps has been formed for people progressing from Stepping Stones. With a focus on worship and teaching done through the prism of interactive family fun, Foot Steps is slowly growing as a worship service for Greengates.

It's still early days, but using the 'serving first' journey, the stages are now set up as Greengates has listened (discerning a need to serve young families), they're building community (Jolly Tots and social nights), exploring discipleship (Stepping Stones) and church is taking shape (Foot Steps), and so this is providing a way for non-churched people to find Jesus and become part of his church.

Whether we are pioneering among young people, city slickers, families, or others who have not spent much time in church, creating a series of stages as a pathway to discipleship and the formation of a Christian community is a great way forward.

Top six reasons for developing stages

1 Stages enable the new church to develop at the *right pace* for the people being reached.
2 Stages enable the new people to move *back and forth*. They frequently move back as well before moving forth as this reflects a process of exploring faith while belonging before believing.
3 Stages enable *significant trust* and belonging to develop between the pioneer team and the new people so that a leap of faith to the next stage is done only when trust has been established.
4 Stages *remove guilt* and the feeling of being judged. It's OK for new people to drop a stage for a while; no one needs to pester them to get back to church before they are ready.
5 Each stage is *valuable and distinctive* in its own right. For example, there is no need to water down the worship service; it can remain faithful to its purpose of providing a space where people can encounter God without worrying that we'll never see the new people again if its 'too Christian'. If some new people aren't ready, they can still belong.

6 It's likely only a few people will be ready for a new stage, but as the stage develops, those new people will become *mini pioneers* to their friends and will draw others in.

Top five tips for developing stages

1 *Take time* to develop each stage properly. Each stage is valuable on its own and needs to be carefully developed over time. It might take a year or two to go from one stage to another. Many seeds will be planted in the earlier stages and this is valuable as an expression of God's kingdom.

2 *Enjoy learning* as you go. Each stage will be a new adventure for your team, so enjoy it, try new things and learn together.

3 When starting a new stage, there must be *continuity* between each stage so that at least some members of the pioneer team travel with the new people into the next stage. This work starts with relationships and should continue with relationships.

4 *Find key new people* and involve them in the planning and running of the next stage. You will then be building Christian community with them, not just for them. It's likely this will help in developing indigenous leadership.

5 *Stages should overlap*, be messy and yet connected. Let each stage keep its distinct focus while being connected. This allows people to move more easily from one stage to another.

Notes

1 Michael Moynagh, *Church for Every Context*, London: SCM Press, 2012, p. 200.
2 Michael Moynagh and Andy Freeman, *How Can Fresh Expressions Emerge?*, Bozeat: Fresh Expresssions, p. 5.
3 Steven Croft, Claire Dalpra and George Lings, *Starting a Fresh Expression*, Bozeat: Fresh Expressions, 2006, p. 3.
4 Mike Breen, *Outside In*, London: Scripture Union, 1993, p. 78.

5

How do I read the context and create opportunities to pioneer?

Get a PhD or get started?

One school of thought within the Fresh Expressions/pioneering/ emerging church scene is that pioneers should spend the first 6–12 months researching the mission context by reading everything available, interviewing and asking people to fill in questionnaires, with the aim of gathering information and gaining as much understanding about the mission context as possible before starting the work. I have named this the 'PhD' approach.

The PhD approach says that failure to go through this research process might cause the team to develop blind spots when surveying the local culture and the needs of its people. It might cause the pioneering team to make big mistakes, such as not making the gospel relevant enough and overlooking people's needs. This places the pioneering work in danger (so says the theory) because it risks failing to connect God to people at their deepest level!

A second school of thought (especially within entrepreneurial writing) I have named the 'get started' approach because the team start pioneering straight away. They learn by engaging with new people in the mission context as they work. 'Start with what you've got: who you are, what you know and who you know.'[1] The idea behind this approach is that pioneers will bring a new reality to birth as they construct the new community, taking both themselves and the new people into a totally new experience. Cultural insights and differences can be learnt and adapted to on the way (as happens with a man and a woman coming together to form a relationship) and so time doesn't need to be wasted doing endless research.

So what should a pioneer do? Get a PhD, get started or get a mix of both? There might be other factors to consider too. You may find that some people want to put time constraints on you. While it's never sensible to rush, you might have team members impatient to see things happen, who will lose motivation and leave if nothing happens for 6–12 months. You might be supported by partners such as local churches that expect to see something happening within 6–12 months. I've experienced both these expectations, and while volunteers and churches had to learn that pioneering takes patience and time, the expectations didn't disappear. So is there a way to deal with the dilemma above without developing blind spots or losing team members and partners because it takes time?

Teenage trends

In early 2003, I knew God was calling us to start a youth church and with six months to go before we made the big move back to Bradford, the whole issue of research was definitely on my mind.

A college course gave me the push to read a whole series of magazines aimed at young people. I deliberately chose magazines that would represent as many different young people as possible. Some magazines were interesting and easy to read while others were obsessed with image and sex in an unhealthy way.

Trying to get beyond the glossy pictures and the push of advertisements, the magazines showed huge differences in the tastes, fashions and interests of different young people. Youth work with young footballers would be different from work with young people into computer gaming. It raised questions. Is it possible to integrate young people from different 'teen tribes' or peer groups into a single fresh expression of church? How do we deal with ongoing conflicts between 'tribes'? Some teen tribes have their own music and don't like the music from other tribes, so does it matter if we develop worship with one style of music or do we need lots of styles? These were some of the questions raised by the magazines. I would have to wait a while to test whether they were important questions or not when working with young people in north Bradford.

Around the same time, I put together a questionnaire to take to young people in Sheffield (where we lived before moving back to Bradford), which would reveal more about the interests, issues and thoughts of young people. The young people being questioned showed some allegiance to the various teen tribes of the time, but many of them could be in two or even three of the tribes or none at all. When asking young people about prayer, belief in God and what they believed about the afterlife, there was some openness and an interest to find out more. While this was a very limited survey, it also suggested that teen tribes weren't as big a deal for some young people as they were for others.

Various books and articles claimed that identity, belonging and friendship were big issues and needs for most young people. Most researchers claimed that a vacuum exists in the UK because young people spend less time with adults than in any other country. Continual reductions in youth work provision by both councils and churches, coupled with the increase of broken families in recent decades, has increased this vacuum of adult nurture so that young people seek to fill it by belonging to a friendship group or tribe while still retaining their own individual identity. So here was my broad research on the lives of young people in the UK. Would it be helpful or would it prove pointless?[2]

As we moved back to Bradford in October 2003, I was told about a piece of research recently carried out by a couple of local YMCA youth workers who compiled the answers of young people to questions such as 'What kind of things do you want in this area?' The most common answer to this question was some variation of 'youth cafe'. It was also noted that there was little youth provision in the area. This research showed there was a lack of suitable spaces and that some young people wanted something to be provided.

Conversations with the school chaplain Stuart Hacking, local Salvation Army youth worker Tony Brown and other local youth workers soon revealed facts and stories about the huge social need across the local area: a school about to go into special measures, young people from two tough council estates with high unemployment, drug and crime issues, and high teenage pregnancy rates. Even in the suburban area, there were similar issues but not as pronounced. The local school was the only thing bringing together young people from across this area.

What was I to do with all this research? I hoped the research might provide the background of a picture that was starting to emerge. Perhaps conversations with local workers and young people might fill in the foreground. My thinking after reflecting on this research was:

- be ready to contextualize the good news into teen tribe language so that it will be heard as relevant by the young hearers
- focus on building relationships with young people who value friendship
- stay close to workers such as the school chaplain, Stuart, and the Salvation Army youth worker, Tony, who know the young people and are already working out how to deal with the social and personal issues.

But I also cautioned myself, 'Don't assume any of this stuff is right but test everything as we go!'

Opportunity recognition[3]

> ### Opportunity recognition
>
> Conversations → See patterns in context → Recognize opportunities → Input into conversations
>
> ### Opportunity creation
>
> Conversations → Make connections in the mind → Test ideals → Create opportunities → Input into conversations

At the time I was having conversations with local workers, I was also chatting with a group of teenage footballers (see Chapter 6) on our street in Eccleshill. A few months earlier, we had looked in different areas at various houses that might be bought for us to live in. Every time we looked at houses in Eccleshill, I sensed in prayer that this was the area in which we should be living. Anyway, we found a suitable house in Eccleshill and this turned out to be a good area for us because there were a lot of young people living on our street and on the next street.

An amazing opportunity to play football with some of the young people came about within two days of our arrival! It really seemed like God had put us in the right place. Little conversations gave us an insight into their lives. There were many social issues, such as lads struggling to live with an alcoholic parent, and a few dysfunctional families. Conversation from these young people was often bite-sized and laced with mistrust. It would take time for the lads to trust me but, by playing football each week, the ice slowly started melting. One lad who had been excluded from school kept knocking at my door and I would chat to him, listen to his problems and repeated requests to borrow money for sweets or cigarettes (none was ever given).

At a recently created youth partnership meeting with councillors and council youth workers, I discovered that a whole set of agencies were setting up short-term programmes to help troubled young people deal with social and personal issues. I soon discovered that the lad knocking on my door was on their list of 'most troubled young people needing a multi-agency approach' to solve his issues.

My gut feeling was to stay quiet and keep talking to this lad, build a relationship with him, with the hope that God would help us form a community where he could belong and then start to solve his problems. My instinctive feeling was that forming a healing, life-giving community where God could minister would be the best solution to these issues. In the meantime, do I start referring young people to these agencies[4] or wait, trusting God to work through his approach? I decided to wait. Although this new community was in the future, everything I said and did had to point towards it and be consistent with its future reality. In other words, I had to be faithful to Jesus and his calling.

Did God want Sorted to be the missing jigsaw piece in a context that needed both youth provision and solutions to young people's issues? At this stage, some of this was joining the dots with what I saw on the ground and yet some of it was sheer faith that God knew what he was doing! Only time would tell whether my faith was misplaced or not.

Opportunity creation

While playing football each week, there were a few other young people on the street who rarely played. Two lads would mountain bike and skateboard. Both were a bit quieter than the others, almost shy. I wondered whether my own interest in skateboarding would be a natural 'way in'.

Spotting the lads while driving past in the car, I decided to take a walk right past them to the local shop. I stopped briefly to ask them about skateboarding and what tricks they could show me. We soon got into a conversation and they invited me to skate with them. Over the next few weeks, I had lots of good conversations with one of these lads called John and this led to other conversations with his peers. Trust came much quicker than with the footballers. The lad prayed and asked God into his life, and a little informal group was formed around him and his peers.

I learnt several things:

- *Building trust and personal relationships* will be very important if we are to form a community.
- Faith conversations revealed how important it is to *contextualize the gospel*. We chatted for an hour about heaven and hell via heavy metal song lyrics on one occasion.
- Our house became a *place of hospitality* where some of these guys came to watch skate DVDs and chat.

Painting a new picture

If we go back to the dilemma outlined at the start of this chapter, we left it with a question: does the pioneer spend 6–12 months doing PhD-style research before beginning to pioneer, or does he or she get started by pioneering immediately?

My experience outlined in the story above suggests the most important thing is to start pioneering and learn as we go through the people we meet. Research formed an important background picture but I learnt mostly through chatting with young people, local workers, trying things, failed experiments and things that worked. The most important thing was to start with me and who God who made me, complete with past experiences, gifts and learning. If God calls you to pioneer something then he's been preparing you for some time. He doesn't make mistakes, so we need to have faith that he has been working in us.

As I got to know young people, I had to learn how to relate to them, I had to learn to understand them and why they said and did things in the way they did. I had to learn what the gospel is for them, how the gospel would become accessible for them and eventually what church would look like for them.

The life stories, needs and issues arising from these encounters can be painted into the foreground of the picture. They should be weighed up against the background research. The encounters with real people and the research can inform each other, ask questions of each other and clarify the pioneer's thinking.

We may ask, 'Do the people in the foreground blend with the scenery in the background or do they seem out of place?' Sometimes the research data will seem out of step with the people being encountered, like a background picture of a hot, sandy beach in Spain with Eskimos clothed in leathers in the foreground. However, the most likely scenario is that as the foreground and background inform and question each other, they enable the pioneer to tweak the picture, sharpen the focus on to what is important and discard what isn't.

As a professional pioneer, I had the opportunity of spending time doing research before the work began, because I was still in theological college. While this was helpful and got me asking the right questions, pioneers who already work in the context, such as someone about to pioneer in their place of work (i.e. school teacher or office worker), will already have knowledge of the people and context simply by having been a part of it. The important thing for them is to ask the right questions of their context and learn from it.

While I had no option but to wait for six months doing research until my job began, those pioneering in their spare time would be better advised to get started, learn as they go by asking questions of the people and context, complementing and testing the learning against good research. As you can see from my questions about teen tribes in Sheffield, the research usually makes more sense when it is compared against real people's lives, but can become confusing and unhelpful when it is left on its own.

Other factors to influence our approach to research

Incarnation

In Luke 2, we read about Jesus' family visit to the Jerusalem Temple and his conversations with the Rabbis. Making regular seasonal visits to the Jewish festivals with his family would have given Jesus a wealth of insight, understanding and experience of the needs of the people he would soon be reaching.

Jesus had immersed himself in the daily life of the people. His incarnational life enabled him to grasp the issues and needs of his hearers. Whether talking to rural peasants through agricultural metaphors about seeds and harvests, or talking to religious Jews through Old Testament verses and temple analogies, Jesus spoke into people's needs using their cultural language. Jesus started with who he was (Son of God, yet also a Palestinian Jew), what he knew (his Father, his country and the culture of his people) and who he knew (his baptism by older cousin John put him in contact with his first disciples).

During my first 18 months back in Bradford, much time was spent simply being with young people in school or hanging out with them in Eccleshill. My experience as a local lad returning home enabled me to connect to the teenagers hanging out in the same places where my mates and I had been 15 years earlier.

Rory Ridley-Duff and Mike Bull write about how social entrepreneurs may temporarily become followers, learning about the culture and needs of the people as they go.[5] There were times during those first 18 months when I felt like a follower of young people!

Before you dismiss me as a dud youth worker, there was method in this madness. It was only by resisting the urge to lead or initiate a new programme that I really learnt to listen to them, make personal connections and understand their issues and concerns. I had to keep my own mouth shut long enough to really hear theirs! There were times during this period when I felt a failure and doubted I was achieving anything. Looking back, much fruit was borne because of this period of listening, learning and connecting, so that when the right time came to initiate and lead I could do so from a foundation of having really understood the culture of the young people.

Context

In the story above, I identify a key young skater called John who became a person of peace (see Jesus' term in Luke 10.6) or networker.[6] Making a personal connection with this lad opened the door to making connections with his peers. Being accepted by him led to me being accepted by his peers.

There was something about the 'person of peace' process that caused the group to allow me in at a deeper level than the footballers, who took much longer to build trust with. Who are the networkers or people of peace in your mission context? These people not only give you a way into a group but they can often teach you a lot about other local people. It might be that you have to follow the lead of such a person for a while to become accepted. How can you follow their lead without losing integrity?

The local workers, such as the school chaplain Stuart, Salvation Army worker Tony, and those who attended the youth partnership meeting, are classed as 'agencies' by Moynagh.[7] They represent the variety of those working among people in the area. While valuable, their information must be tested and weighed as each person is likely to 'see' things through both the lens of their experience and their particular speciality. For example, the council youth workers had useful insights when it came to befriending and being aware of the social needs of local young people, yet their only preconceived solution was a multi-agency approach of professional help ministered in one-to-one meetings of an adult to a young person. Although I wanted to learn and work with the agencies, those workers couldn't consider the impact that a Spirit-filled community could have in bringing transformation to young lives. Many professionals were stuck in a provider–client model of help and could never grasp what might happen if the young people truly 'owned' and became committed to this new Jesus-centred community. Healing and transformation might come through this new community as young people take ownership and give themselves to each other and to God.

An interview with a Church Army project leader in the North of England[8]

Working with vulnerable women, many with addictions and a life of prostitution, one question is – How are they reached by the gospel and how is community formed in such tough contexts?

'We try and deal with the whole person. For example, we visit a woman addicted to heroin twice a week. Her addiction causes her to despair of life and go without food so we feed her and offer her a bath, showing the love of a family to her, gently encouraging her to talk to Jesus . . . Jesus himself often dealt with the immediate needs of the person such as the woman with bleeding who first needed healing as she touched the hem of his garment.'

'We've visited a woman with chronic alcohol addiction for nine years. One day, we were surprised to find her telling us, "Come and meet my prayer group . . . God is still with me even though I drink." She had seen us praying down the years and decided to begin her own group among her friends.'

A team member summed up their approach to context and community:

'It's better for us to enter their world; if we tried to take them out of it, it would destroy them and their relationships in the process; Jesus spent all his time in sinners' environments. The women have loving friendships that aren't perfect but who's to say their love is not from God; we must go to them, journey with them, be family with them and their community.'

Reroute in Bulgaria

We were on holiday at a friend's house in Bulgaria. We had been shopping in the nearby city of Veliko Tarnovo, about eight miles from her home. Travelling back in the dark on the only main road home from Veliko Tarnovo, we hit a traffic jam. Minutes earlier, a car had crashed and we were now stuck in a queue. About 40 minutes later, we had only moved three or four metres and the cars in front of us were turning round and driving back towards the city.

Our friend Emma had been living in Bulgaria for a few years. She knew that there would be another way to get home via local villages but signposts and maps are primitive in this part of Bulgaria and so we needed help. Emma hastily rang up a Bulgarian friend named Hristo who advised a new route to the south via three tiny villages to bypass the traffic block. With Emma's home only a mile away, this surely wouldn't take long.

Setting off down a side road into the first village, we came to a fork in the road ahead with no signposts to guide us. A local man gave us directions but we still seemed to get lost. It was dark and misty and there was no chance of finding our bearings by looking in the distance for landmarks. Emma still thought she knew where to go and so we kept going. Within a few minutes we found ourselves going out of the village and up a hill in the countryside. Surely the next village was just over the hill?

We steadily climbed up and up the hill. The mist was growing thicker and thicker and we were rising higher still. Something wasn't right; we should have found the next village by now!

Tracy stepped out of the car and immediately noticed how cold it was. Standing near the edge of the narrow road, she realized that we were very high up a mountain and there were big drops down both sides just beyond the edges of the road. We had no option but to do what seemed like a 20-point turn in the narrow road (being careful to avoid the edge of the road) and go back to the village on the same road.

Back down in the village, Emma made another phone call to Hristo and we set off again. We eventually arrived home after two hours of detours. If there had not been an accident, it would have literally taken five minutes on the main road but at least we made it home!

Reroute

So imagine you've read how other pioneers have done it, you've done your research and got to know a few local people, but suddenly the ideas you started with don't seem to fit what you're seeing on the ground. The vision is still the same but the way to reach your destination is more unclear than ever. What do you do?

Many of us start with a few ideas or even a plan of action but then find that it's not as straightforward as we expected. The ideas don't work or the starting point is different from what we imagined. This can be a moment of real crisis, confusion or even panic, especially if our plans were fairly fixed. We need to rethink our next move.

When our road of travel has roadblocks in the way, we need to look at the map and reroute! The *Oxford Dictionary* says that to reroute is to 'send by or along a different route'.[9] When we were driving up the mountain in Bulgaria and getting lost, it was frustrating to reroute, but continuing in the same direction might have been disastrous. There are times when we hit a roadblock in pioneering and, despite the frustration and reluctance to change direction, it's sometimes right to step back from a situation and be prepared to reroute.

The roadblock! Our first crisis!

Throughout 2003 and early 2004, I had spent time researching the context, interviewing local workers and gaining insights from conversations with young people. I quickly formed a basic plan of action and shared it with the volunteer team I was meeting to train with each Friday night.

The initial plan went something like this:

1 Do schools work, look for people of peace and build relationships with them.
2 Organize a meeting where the young people of peace will meet the volunteer team.
3 Put together two adults with two young people to form a mini group; this group will grow as the two young people invite their friends.
4 Let each mini group meet weekly for activities and discussion; everything should be planned with the young people.
5 While young people choose the activities, the adults' role is to relate, care, share faith and enable the group to run smoothly. Young people will hear the gospel, some will come to faith and we will form a youth congregation later on.

Roadblock 1

While this plan had lots of good things, we hit our first road-block immediately at part 2! The young people we were getting to know in school had never met as a group outside school and were unlikely to attend a one-off session. Inviting them to the session might attract a few but not many. Also, we couldn't do the session in school because the adult volunteers were at work during school hours.

I wasn't convinced the young people would partner with the volunteers to lead mini groups because they didn't yet know them. We were discovering that building trust with these young people takes time. I soon knew that my carefully worked-out plan might be doomed before it even started. I needed to reroute.

Roadblock 2

My revised plan would allow time for volunteers and young people to build trust. Starting with detached youth work in the local area, I encouraged the volunteers to build relationships with young people they met at street corners and in local parks. We would then form small groups when these relationships became stronger.

Within a few weeks of doing detached work, it became obvious this plan was unlikely to work. Although one or two volunteers adapted well to detached work, most were way out of their comfort zone and unable to approach groups of young people sitting in bus shelters or on park benches. It says a lot about the team that they were prepared to go along with my crazy idea for as long as they did.

During the detached work, God began to interrupt things. As we worshipped and prayed before walking the streets, I kept getting the sense that instead of sending out ten adults in pairs (my way), Robert (who adapted well to detached work) and I should go alone (God's way). At first this didn't make sense: how could the volunteers get to know the young people and start the groups if we did it this way? Like Jacob wrestling with

God, I started my own wrestle with God – some weeks we did it my way and some weeks we did it his way. Eventually, God won the wrestling match as it became obvious that it worked better when Robert and I went on our own!

Roadblock 3

While talking this over with others, two friends separately suggested that I should do the detached work with Robert alone and set up just one group! This group could act as a prototype before other groups were set up. While I could see the logic of their idea, I still had big concerns. Suppose this idea worked? How would I be able to get the volunteers to do the same thing later on?

As it happened, Robert and I had recently set up a small group that met each Wednesday at 4 p.m. (see the story in Chapter 6), but the young people hadn't come through the Friday-night detached work but through a young person I'd got to know in the school playground. This gave me an idea.

What if the way out of this pioneering maze was to be found by forming one prototype group from school contacts, not from the detached work? It could start on a Friday night; we would then grow it bigger, bringing the adult team alongside it so that relationships could form. I hoped this would eventually lead to the formation of the small groups. This would turn out to be a eureka moment, even if I couldn't see it at the time.

Roadblock 4

By autumn 2004, I was desperate to get something up and running. I was getting impatient and so were my superiors, who didn't seem all that interested in my comments about roadblocks and pioneering mazes! I'm not sure they believed in them, and to be honest nor did I. Nevertheless, we now started thinking about venues for a large group and what activities might be needed. The local YMCA research mentioned earlier in the chapter pointed to a youth cafe. Young people sitting round tables would give us an opportunity to chat with them and ask them what kind of activities they would like to do. Groups might be formed later on.

While praying in early November with a team member, I had the tiniest sense that God was saying Easter. It was so quiet that I really wasn't sure it was God; anyway, it couldn't be God because Easter was six months away, and I was hoping to have this started within a few weeks!

As the weeks progressed, with no obvious venue and my stress levels increasing, the local youth partnership meeting of counsellors and youth workers came up with an idea for a metal portacabin, or POD, to be placed in the local area for multiple users. This idea had come up in discussions a few times, but it was only a serious contender by the autumn of 2004. By December, we were told the POD was on its way and the council youth services would organize who could use it and when! After the previous roadblocks, I had my doubts. Would a small POD be sufficient? How could we do youth cafe in it? It wasn't what I had in mind and so I wasn't overly optimistic!

In January we were offered use of the POD and I asked for Friday nights. Reluctantly I felt that we had to give this a try. By February, I got a phone call from the local council youth worker asking me to come and help as the POD was to be lowered by a crane into the top corner of the school grounds. Within a few days, the POD had landed. It was leaning on a slope, grubby on the inside and had no electricity, which meant there were no lights and so it was unusable until the nights became light.

By Easter 2005, the nights were just about light enough for us to use the POD between 6 and 8 p.m. We had a venue and it was in the very school grounds where I was doing detached work! Now it was time to put the latest plan in motion and test it out.

I was so used to roadblocks, and lacking in belief that we were remotely near succeeding, that I started the POD doubting myself, expecting another roadblock just around the corner. What followed would blow our brains and change all of our perceptions for good! I later realized we had been training in the dark for a marathon we didn't know was just about to start. It was like leaving the maze to stand at the starting line.

For the next few years, we would run hard and fast as each phase of the race became both more demanding and immensely more rewarding. We would discover gifts, abilities and energies that we never knew we had as God led us into the fulfilment of our mission fantasies!

Making sense of rerouting – how to do it

Our story involved loads of rerouting. Don't be put off – for most fresh expressions it's not as extreme. As a rule, the more chaotic and unpredictable a mission context is, the more rerouting there is likely to be. The less chaotic and unpredictable a mission context is, the less rerouting there is likely to be.[10]

Within the story above, it's possible to identify several tools that a pioneer can use to reroute when overcoming road-blocks so that he or she can still reach their destination. Mike Moynagh identifies seven such tools or aids to reflection.[11]

1 Observation

For me, observation of young people in north Bradford showed me that my initial plan was going to fail. Yet by observing how long it took to build trust and the need to build a group on the foundation of the relationships being developed, we also started to realize some of the key ingredients that would be needed to make a plan work.

Write down your observations of the people you're seeking to reach, especially when it comes to how they act socially and their attitudes to outsiders. Pray and ask questions of your observations and talk them over with others. Journalling observations and testing them out with others is a great way to keep learning about those you want to reach.

- What are the strongly held beliefs of the people you meet?
- How has their background taught them to behave?
- What do they regard as major offences to their moral code?
- What do they do in a crisis?

- Who are the most influential people?
- What are their greatest fears?
- What is considered to be wisdom and who are the wisdom-givers?
- What is expressed in the art forms of their culture?
- What aspects of their culture are most resistant to change?[12]

Your observations may both pleasantly surprise and confuse you. There will be times when your observations inform your work in obvious ways and other times when they seem meaningless. My advice is to persevere in recording your observations. Ask God to open the eyes of your heart (Ephesians 1.18) to notice so much more than you would otherwise see through using the discipline of observation.

2 Conversation

Sharing observations can help test out what we're thinking and help us to make more sense of what we are seeing. It also encourages other team members to see, observe and contribute to the ongoing conversation.

'Innovative entrepreneurs were more likely to ask questions that challenged the status quo . . . e.g. if we do this, what will happen?'[13] Conversations often lead to ideas and creative thinking outside the box. When two friends separately told me that Robert and I should do detached work alone and then form a prototype group, this confirmed what we thought God was saying and caused us to start thinking differently and creatively about how things might work. It was a key insight that we would later benefit from as the POD sessions started.

3 Experimentation

Many famous inventors and scientists tell stories of dozens of failed experiments. Thomas Edison famously had 10,000 failed experiments before inventing the light bulb. We experienced a relatively small number of roadblocks and reroutes in the story above by comparison.

When asked if he felt like a failure, Edison replied perplexedly, 'Young man, why would I feel like a failure? And why would I ever give up? I now know definitively over 9,000 ways that an electric light bulb will not work. Success is almost in my grasp.'[14] Edison learnt more through failure than through success.

In most failed pioneering ventures there will be much that can be learnt. I learnt not to send out ten volunteers to do detached work but to send out a couple of people gifted to do it. It messed up my plans, but it was a lesson I needed to learn.

4 *Participation*

By participating in the lives of those they are called to reach, team members identify with the new people, gain insights by researching real lives, and build relationships. In Luke 10, Jesus sent his 72 followers to participate in people's lives by sending them in pairs to local towns and villages.

But reality strikes! We struggled to follow the example of the 72 followers, hitting roadblock after roadblock when we tried to get our team members to participate in the everyday lives of the young people. The young people and the adults just didn't naturally mix. Most adults tend to avoid and even fear 'hoodie type' groups of young people hanging out on street corners, while most young people mistrust adults they don't know.

In contexts where there is a big cultural gap between the team and the new people, forming connections between the two groups can require lots of creative thinking. But in many other contexts, where it's much more natural for team members to mingle with the people they are called to, it should be much easier. For example, community social spaces such as pubs, cafes or libraries might be spaces that allow team members to socialize with the new people. Joining a gym, a school governing body, line dancing, a local reading group or a self-help group such as weight watchers are just a few ways to make those connections and start participating.

KEY INSIGHT – pioneers may need to form connections in pairs until a 'way in' to the people group has been found so that other team members can 'piggy back' on to the new connections and start participating themselves.

I had to make the connections with one other team member initially (or alone in the playground while staying in the eyesight of other adults) until a bridge had been established to the young people. Once relationships and trust were being established, other team members could cross the bridge. Going in pairs makes it much easier to fit in, adapt to the cultural norms and be accepted – that's probably why Jesus didn't send the 72 in eights or nines but in pairs! So if you're a pioneer, go in a pair, listen and learn to fit in, observe what's going on and adapt your approach to the people so you can build relationships and establish trust.

5 Investigation

We had to investigate what venues were available to us and what we were capable of doing. For a while, we investigated whether it was possible to buy an old bus, renovate it and use it as mobile youth provision. Fortunately, the local youth partnership was also investigating whether a bus, building or POD was the best way to find a venue to run youth sessions.

'If you run a session in the POD, are you planning on using a Bible?' asked the head youth worker before agreeing to let us use it. The local youth partnership was full of people with good intentions, but some had their reservations about Christianity. I never quite knew whether we would be included when a venue was found. Looking back, I'm pretty sure the local councillors wanted us included and would have made sure we were given a chance to use the venue. Investigation means taking calculated risks that something will come off, but there are no guarantees. Building relationships with local agencies and workers is likely to open doors.

6 Corporate alertness

Throughout the process of listening, researching, planning, hitting roadblocks and rerouting, there were conversations happening between myself and local partners, workers, agencies and young people. These conversations were relayed to Tracy on a daily basis (poor wife!), and individuals in the team, via phone or text during the week. Ideas and plans were formulated and then shared with the whole team each Friday and their feedback was listened to.

Having conversations with different team members, hearing their viewpoints and involving them in the process made us a real team. Collective wisdom was gained and we all grew a little closer to each other and came to a closer understanding of what God was calling us to do. Conversations increased commitment in many team members. This was the only authentic way that a community could make decisions. Yet at the same time, I led the decision-making process because leadership was needed to guide and help us get to the point of decision-making and taking action.

7 How might a vision emerge?

As the team discovered new insights through observation, God's guidance and the comments of two friends, these insights had to be assimilated into our thinking and formulated into a new plan. This process took a while. The team had to go through a period of 'letting go' of the initial plan, needed space to come to terms with the new idea before working out how to put it into action. This certainly wasn't easy. As we began carrying out the new idea, our resources had to change and adapt to fit it.

Notes

1 Michael Moynagh, *Being Church, Doing Life: Creating Gospel Communities where Life Happens*, Oxford: Monarch, 2014, p. 45.
2 Although I undertook this research in 2003, most of the underlying factors mentioned above have changed very little since then.

3 Michael Moynagh, *Church for Every Context*, London: SCM Press, 2012, p. 251.

4 The central thrust of our work is to journey with young people but we do refer young people to various agencies when it would best help them.

5 Rory Ridley-Duff and Mike Bull, *Understanding Social Enterprise: Theory and Practice*, London: Sage, 2011, p. 207.

6 Moynagh, *Church for Every Context*, p. 254.

7 Moynagh, *Church for Every Context*, p. 254.

8 The names and places are kept anonymous to protect the people involved.

9 See Oxford Dictionary at http://www.oxforddictionaries.com.

10 See Moynagh, *Church for Every Context* (p. 199) for an explanation of simple, chaotic, complicated and complex contexts.

11 Moynagh, *Church for Every Context*, p. 199.

12 Questions adapted from Mike Breen, *Outside In*, London: Scripture Union, 1993, p. 10.

13 Moynagh, *Church for Every Context*, p. 260.

14 Thomas Edison, https://www.goodreads.com/author/quotes/3091287.Thomas_A_Edison.

PART 3

Making it happen – getting stuck in

6

Where do I love and serve people, and how do I build community?

The POD story

'Have you ever seen the POD that they use on the *X Factor*? Yeah, that's right – the metal portacabin they use to interview people in different cities up and down the UK', went a typical conversation as I explained to young people about the 'building' where our Friday-night session would happen. Sorted really took off when we started meeting in the POD. Not a trendy *X Factor* POD with bright lights in a flashy shopping centre with an *X Factor* logo painted on the side of it. Our POD was dirty, smelly and had recently been lowered by crane on to a gentle slope that could make you feel seasick if you thought about it too much. Its electric generator would break down and stop working, causing its lights to switch off, plunging the group into darkness right in the middle of one of my talks! But despite its problems, this was the POD we were given to use and this was where God birthed Sorted into life. Here's how it happened.

During October 2004, two prophetic things happened. We knew we needed a place to gather together the young people we had got to know and also get Sorted known among other local young people. As I explained this to a mentor, he said to me, 'Just do it, just do it, just do it [and, in case I hadn't got the message], just do it, just do it, just do it.' The following night I was sitting trying to stay awake during our monthly prayer meeting. A woman had a picture from God, of the Nike logo, and said, 'God wants you to "just do it".' Wow! This woman knew nothing of the conversation I'd had with my friend the day before. Here was one of those wow moments where God was speaking very clearly to me.[1] I figured I had better just do it!

Simon and Val are amazing couple who joined Sorted right at the start as volunteers, and have been with us ever since. Two weeks later, I was praying with Val, asking God to provide a place we could use to hold a weekly youth session. I had the faintest sense that God was saying the session would start the following Easter but I soon dismissed this as not being of God because it seemed such a long way off (as I mentioned briefly in Chapter 5).

There was no obvious place to hold a weekly youth work session. The only youth facility in the area had recently shut down and no one seemed to be willing to allow us to bring young people 'off the streets' into their building due to a fear of vandalism. It seemed as though every door we tried was firmly shut, locked and padlocked! But a new year brought a new opportunity – at least it did eventually. A plan was under-way to put a metal portacabin in the grounds of the secondary school that could be used by the local youth services, by the school and other youth work providers. We came under the last category.

Things seemed to be coming together – I asked the youth services if we could use the POD on Friday nights because this was the night our adult team already met. It was also the night we had sensed God giving us in prayer. We figured out that Friday night would be a good night to run the session because few young people were in doing homework (we soon discovered that at that time, no one in Sorted did homework anyway) as might be the case earlier in the week, and some young people would be away visiting dad on a Saturday night (this predic-tion did prove accurate). The local youth services were only too happy for us to do Friday nights – in one youth worker's opinion, this was the night most young people would get drunk and that made it a waste of time to do youth work.

Eventually, after months of waiting for the generator because it was too dark to use the POD without electric lights during winter, the UK's clocks moved forward by an hour at the end of March and we had enough light to start a session at 6 p.m. This happened one week after Easter as God had said it would do!

Young people arrive slowly

In the run-up to Easter, I had started telling young people about the Friday-night sessions we were going to have at the POD. I was certain we would have a great turnout of people for our first night.

The following Friday, just Simon and I were at the POD, waiting for the crowds to arrive. The other team members had stayed at the primary school to pray with Tracy so that there weren't too many adults hanging around to put new young people off. At 6.30 I was getting worried because no one had turned up. At 6.35 three lads arrived; surely this was the start of many more arrivals? We chatted with them about all sorts of stuff, waiting to see if anyone would show up, but no one did.

One week later, Simon and I were ready waiting hopefully for a group to arrive at 6 p.m. A little later, one of the three lads from the previous week arrived. We chatted to him for ages, but no one else showed up that night. I started to worry that the whole thing might not work out; this led to a very persistent prayer life for a while! During this time, a wise friend said to me, 'Keep telling the young people about the session regularly and don't even look at the number of people attending until at least a month has passed.' It proved to be good advice because the following week, after conversations in the school and in Eccleshill, around eight young people arrived and we spent the evening skateboarding and chatting. We all had a good night! It seemed we might be turning a corner.

From the end of April through to July, almost every Friday night seemed to have good weather. This really helped us because the grounds of the school were good for skateboarding, football and hanging out. As the weeks went by, more and more young people started coming down, so that the numbers were in the mid 20s by July. As numbers of young people steadily grew, we carefully increased the number of team members, transferring them to the POD from the primary school, so that by July the whole team were at the POD. Some young people came from our contacts in school, others came from contacts in Eccleshill, and they all brought their friends.

After what had seemed like an eternity, we had found ourselves with a good number of young people. Most of them came to the POD to skateboard, play football or to simply hang out with their mates. How could we get them connected to God and how could God form a church from this group?

Tony and I were taking it in turns to do a short talk halfway through the session. (It had to be at the halfway point because a significant number would try to avoid the talk by arriving late or leaving early.) Making the peer pressure work in our favour was crucial. We didn't have strong relationships with any of the group at this stage so if we'd allowed them to miss the talk, the whole crowd might easily have gone. We had no other choice but to insist that for 90% of the session, they were free to do as they pleased, but for a few short minutes each week, we insisted that they hear the talk. We used quizzes, DVD clips, testimonies, games and discussion as a way of getting the young people to think about God and to consider inviting him into their lives. On the whole, it was hard work! Keeping some young people quiet while we talked was a constant battle – even for a few minutes.

At the start of each session, we would ask, 'What do you want to do?' If some young people chose to play football, we would ask them to organize their own game. Two adults would play as well, to make sure the game was being run fairly, but the young people took ownership of the game. All activities would aim to involve the young people, giving them ownership.

Although we had one lad who decided to become a Christian, most young people seemed uninterested in God (eventually I realized that God or Christianity seemed 'uncool' to them and so negative peer pressure was at work). It would take patience and time until things changed.

As we started to meet up again at the end of summer, a chat involving one girl called Rachel and my wife Tracy led to both of them deciding to pray about a personal issue that Rachel was facing. They waited until the end of the evening, and then they prayed in the POD. Things must have gone well because they decided to pray again at the end of the following Friday night with Val and two more girls.

Within a couple of weeks, I started inviting a few more young people to stay behind and pray in little groups of four or five around gas lanterns. The gas lanterns seemed to give just enough light so that it didn't feel like we were all blindfolded. It also felt private so that the young people felt confident enough to pray without others laughing at them. Pretty soon, two-thirds of the main group were choosing to stay behind to pray. This was another example of God using Tracy's creative spontaneity, while I saw the potential and tried to build on what was happening.

I had to find a simple format to enable prayer to happen. We would go round in a group of four or five getting everyone to think of one thing they or someone close to them might need prayer for, then we would go round and each pray silently or aloud for the person next to us. I really felt the sense of God's presence one night as we prayed, and God really blessed quite a few young people on those nights.

Throughout these first months, we were loving and serving young people, being intentional in doing evangelism and starting to see the first signs of a community emerging.

Ways to be intentional when doing evangelism[2]

Pioneers must be intentional when it comes to evangelism, prayerfully seeking what God is doing, reflecting carefully on what types of evangelism might work in the mission context and then working with others to make it happen. There is likely to be a lot of trial and error, a need to take risks, a parable of the sower lens on results, willingness to learn from mistakes and trust that God is working through the whole process.

Reframing conversations

Mike Moynagh[3] writes about the importance of really understanding how God, Christianity, the team and any evangelistic interventions are being perceived by the people being reached. This understanding can give us key insights so that our evangelistic conversations and/or talks are reframed to be as relevant as possible to the people we meet.

Nick Lebey came to us from Church Army via Ghana, South Africa and Northern Ireland. He spent four years training with us in Bradford before moving to pioneer a youth church called TYM in south London using the Sorted model. When running a small group with half a dozen football-mad boys, Nick asked the boys, 'Is God more like the referee, best player, manager or a crowd member?' Next day, Nick rang me to say he had the best discussion ever with those boys who really engaged with the question, exploring in depth what God might be like. It's conversations like these that can spark future ideas for evangelism. What issues and interests might you create evangelistic conversations around?

Acts of kindness

Acts of kindness show God's love to people and are often reciprocated as love gives birth to love. If acts of kindness can become a natural part of a community then this gives an opportunity for new people to be generous, find contentment by knowing that they are helping others and live a little closer to the heart of God.

Some of our boys learnt to bring and share packets of biscuits. Some people clean up gardens, offer support to older people, volunteer to work with children or clean off graffiti. There are limitless ways to do acts of kindness, but by doing it together it gives people the opportunity who wouldn't step out on their own.

Acts of kindness should be modelled by the team so that a new community can practise them – but herein lies a potential danger. When charities give aid to developing countries they face the problem that a well-intentioned gift of aid might create a dependency culture among the recipients. This was a problem for the old western missionaries in Africa too. Pioneering teams need to 'wise up' in how they do acts of kindness so they don't create unhealthy 'dependency' relationships.

At one of our earliest youth sessions, a Christian volunteer wanted to give free chocolate and Pepsi to young people with no money. This gave us a dilemma – my heartstrings said let's give away freebies as an act of kindness, but my head wondered, 'Will they come back every week and expect the same thing free of charge?' Doing freebies now and again is OK and we decided that Sorted would only give out freebies during occasional celebrations such as a Christmas or end-of-term party. Individual team members might decide to buy a drink or a chocolate bar for a young person with no money, but as a team we make sure this stays an act of kindness and doesn't become a weekly expectation. This works well – team members show kindness while young people don't develop unhealthy dependency relationships.

Working in areas of low income, dependency on benefits and high unemployment can increase the danger of dependency. Sorted has had to fundraise to take young people from low-income families away to summer camp or Soul Survivor festivals. The danger of dependency isn't just with young people; some parents see this as an opportunity to 'get the kids away for a week on a freebie'.

In our experience, the key to solving all this 'dependency' stuff is building a good relationship with the people where honest conversations can happen. Good relationships give people the chance to see that we are being generous, that the organization isn't loaded with money and that we are doing what we can to help them. Both parents and young people can be asked to contribute what they can, gentle bartering can take place and the relationship will be strengthened and they will be appreciative.

God-talk

Whether in a school assembly or lunch club, interview in a cafe, during live music (in cafe/club/pub) or at a community event, it's possible to find ways of talking about God. Prayer, content, context and approach are all important. Using these opportunities to creatively tell stories of God at work, which are both relevant to the audience, authentic, personal and yet implicitly challenge the unbelieving world view of the listeners, are key elements.

During a school assembly, I retold the story of the Good Samaritan as the story of the Good Mosher (a group of young people in the school into rock or heavy metal music often belittled by others). Using local street names, events natural to the pupils, such as waiting for a parent to pick up and a mobile phone out of credit, the mosher became the good guy. The listeners were unsure whether my story was true or invented until the end when I linked it to the Good Samaritan. It created conversations, challenged the stereotypical view of moshers and got people asking questions about the guy who told the original story.

Missional worship

Once again, the mission context is everything. Suddenly introducing a worship band and expecting non-churched working people to join in is likely to embarrass or put off people who probably never sing in public unless they are at a football match! But the same scenario might work in a middle-class rural area with middle-aged dechurched people who enjoy singing as a pastime.

There are now so many styles of contemporary Christian music that could be used as a prelude to a God talk or to provide a quiet act of worship in a side room next to a cafe or community space.

Short, sensitive acts of worship using candles and semi-darkness can be good optional extras to a community event. Use of silence, short relevant liturgies and prayer can provide opportunities for people to open up to spiritual things, truth about God and to encounter the Spirit.

Answered prayer

How do we start natural conversations about Jesus with people who are not asking questions about faith, without forcing the issue? As well as reframing conversations and doing acts of kindness, look for opportunities to pray for a person's need. So often, a short prayer for a person in need can lead to an answered prayer and a person opening up to God.

One day I was on the phone to a parent for the first time. This parent worked out I'm a Christian from my job, and I think that's why she started telling me about her visits to a spiritualist church to seek help with a problem. Sensing a natural opportunity, I tested the water by sharing a very brief testimony of how I had prayed for someone and God had given them his peace. To my surprise, she was genuinely interested, so I offered to pray for her. Experience told me that these opportunities are often lost if they aren't taken when they happen, so I prayed aloud down the phone, we waited in silence for a few minutes and then she described an experience of the Holy Spirit.

Creative expressions of spirituality

Offering spiritual support for people needing healing in a local shopping mall or town centre, an environment project with prayers, or offering counselling with prayers, are just a few ideas that have been used as ways to engage people with spirituality. Most of these ideas start by identifying a need that God can meet, and then creatively offering a service to meet this need, which includes practical help and spiritual support.

Using lantern light, small groups and one-word prayers was our way of trying to create something that would give shy teenagers with no experience of church a way to connect with God and express spirituality in the POD.

The Living Room and Franky's Pizza – by Tina Powsey[4]

'We hand delivered Franky's Pizza leaflets to 340 homes; James knocked on doors and a number of conversations took place which demonstrated great interest in Franky's. As a result of one of those conversations, a woman joined us with her young granddaughter from the local school and they had a wonderful time. They promised to come again and bring some friends along too.

The vision for Franky's is to create sustainable relationships on the Kew Estate that will develop into living relationships with Jesus Christ. I recognize the "belonging before belief" mentality and that's exactly what we hope to achieve at Franky's Pizza – fun, food, conversation and God at the centre of it all.

The Living Room, the community which has developed from the ministry of a soup kitchen, has seen great developments too. We are still seeing a steady attendance and I've been having progressive conversations with one of our guests who is now seeking baptism. We've got such a strong sense of community there; it's an absolute honour to bring God's Word to them in a way that's accessible so that they can know what Jesus meant when he talked about having life in abundance – and that knowledge makes such a difference to people. I see that displayed in various ways; sometimes their countenance changes, they walk a little taller, display more confidence, welcome in the stranger and have concern for each other.'

Conversations on the doorstep through visiting homes to drop off leaflets and forming Franky's Pizza so that new people can share in food and fun has been a great way to love and serve people on the Kew Estate. Adding to the loving and serving already being done via a soup kitchen, this has been a great way to begin forming a fresh expression of church and a great example of loving and serving in another context.

Building community

During those first months at the POD, an event was organized by the council for local youth groups. Looking back, we were only two months into the POD so I should have declined the invitation. Instead, eager to promote Sorted, I went off to the event with three young people and a team member. After escaping early, we arrived back at the POD to discover it had been a difficult night.

It's not that there were too many young people at the POD that night; it's not that there was a major cause of conflict; in many ways it was a normal youth session. Young people misbehaved and adults responded in ways they knew best but there wasn't yet enough care, respect, love and shared purpose in our group to resolve issues quickly and move on. At this point, we were still a crowd, not a community. On other weeks, fragile relationships held together because I'd got to know the young people a little bit better through schools work, but remove the pioneer for one night and it could all go pear-shaped very quickly!

This highlights a common pioneering issue. Whether it's young people misbehaving, adult apathy or all-age consumers unwilling to lift a finger to help, the symptoms all point to one underlying problem – how does a pioneering team start to see a 'crowd' become a 'community'?

A crowd becoming a community

I got to know Ben in school. With skateboarding as a common factor, we soon gelled. Even before the POD, Ben hinted that he and his mates would get involved in Sorted when it began.

Around the same time as the difficult night described above, Sorted was reviewed by the diocese and Church Army. During a visit to our tiny Wednesday small group, my boss sensed something positive going on. After Ben and his mate James had gone home, he said, 'That's where your youth church is going to come from, from those two lads, not from the crowd in the POD!' It's hard to put your finger on exactly what caused him to say this but something about the respect levels, shared sense of purpose, mutual care and openness to God caused him to see the seed of a community.

A month later, Ben and I started a small group for his mates that would meet each Tuesday night to 'chill and chat' – spend time chatting about God or a life issue and spend time chilling together over computer games, skateboarding or basketball (see Chapter 7).

Ben and James were influential young people in this group; it was their mates who came regularly to it. A strong sense of purpose, openness to God, respect for me and Robert or Richard (alternating adults), plus Ben's willingness to let us meet in his house, were all factors that caused the group to function as a mini community. Although far from perfect, values like hospitality, care and concern, spirituality, empowerment and openness to newcomers were all present. So each week we had a crowd on Fridays in the POD and a mini community on Tuesdays. I desperately wished I could inject some of the Tuesday group's values into the Friday-night crowd. But, to be truthful, I didn't have a clue if or how this could be done – so we just prayed instead!

The weird thing was that people in the Tuesday group didn't attend Fridays. This slowly started to change. Ben and James were great lads but, like all young people, they could have their moments. Would they be influenced the wrong way by the 25 people at the POD, or could we get Ben and

James and others from Tuesdays to positively influence the 25 people at the POD?

Between the summers of 2005 and 2006, we found ourselves with five mini groups of between two and six people per group. Our aim in forming these groups was to build deeper relationships with people from the POD and share our faith. Some groups were informal and purely conversational, because that's the only thing the young people wanted, while others such as the Tuesday group included time for God.

We didn't advertise these groups, they came about organically as relationships grew and people wanted to meet up beyond the POD. New young people started joining the Tuesday and Wednesday groups. The Tuesday mini community grew and newcomers caught their values, so that some newcomers would bring a packet of biscuits or drinks to share.

In September 2006, we formed a group to plan and start a youth worship service (see Chapter 8). Most young people came from the mini community meeting on Tuesdays and Wednesdays. The mini community began growing as it added other adults and young people. Still, how would we get the values of this community injected into the larger Friday group, which had now moved into the local Methodist church building?

In December 2006, I spent one difficult Friday night chasing a small number of young people who kept trying to nip out of the session to smoke cannabis. We now had 40 attending most weeks, but I was spending all my time dealing with behavioural issues and neglecting guys like Ben and James who now came every week. Something had to change.

In January 2007, we decided to take a risk. The Methodist building had four decent-sized rooms so we decided to split the 40 young people into four groups of eight young people, plus two young leaders leading each group with adult support. After chatting, amending and agreeing the new plan with the whole Friday group, we then trained up young people from the mini community to be the young leaders.

We began the format as young people chose a group to join; each group did a simple Bible discussion together, prayed and then chose a group activity for the night. We had a room to do indoor sports, use of the school grounds, AV equipment and other resources, so groups could swap rooms depending on what they wanted to do. The idea was to try and take the members of the mini community and empower them as young leaders to inject the mini community's values directly into the main artery of Fridays!

Six months later we stopped the experiment because it was impossible to keep the young people caged in one room. This was severely restricting what activities they could do. However, the experiment had been a brilliant evangelism tool because young leaders told their peers how they had seen prayers answered or experienced God through our worship service. God-talk had multiplied among the young people and many in the Friday crowd began asking lots of questions and exploring faith.

Over time we could see the injection had provided a boost! The Friday group began making the transition from crowd to community; the young leaders stayed together and continued running the Friday session with the adults, even after the 'four group' experiment ended. Many of the values of the mini community were caught by those in the Friday crowd and that influence stayed.

There were other practical changes we made to our Friday session that helped create community, as I will explain below.

Crowd or community – how do we get from crowd to community?

We start with a vision of what kind of community we want to be. Using the example of Israel in the Old Testament, Moynagh[5] explains how Christian community should be hospitable, open to outsiders, foster solidarity, disperse power, be relevant to everyday life and foster a community identity. Our contextualized visions of community should connect and resonate with this vision of community from Scripture.

We then need to find others to share this vision of community with. It's essential that when pioneers form a team, the team members begin to catch the vision and practise being community together. We do training sessions with our team and organize prayer breakfasts and/or socials to both share a vision of community and to practise it. It's only after we've done this that we have any form of community worth modelling to outsiders.

When the POD session started, big numbers of young people, together with the age gap between teenagers and our team aged 40–55, meant that creating community would be more challenging. The story above shows how we had to work through really small groups in order to create a mini community, first with two people, then with six people, then ten and then twelve young people before we could influence the bigger group effectively.[6]

If your biggest group shows symptoms of being a crowd, the best strategy for transforming a crowd into a community is to form a small group of people who are open to the vision of community. Teach and practise community, then empower them to be influential within the bigger group by involving them in running it. They could become helpers, plan events or simply be encouraged to be a helpful presence within the bigger group.

Search for ways to deepen relationships and build trust with people in the crowd. The stages model of fresh expressions can really help because if you meet a new person in a pub, then you meet them as they attend a social group and then a small group, your relationship with the person will deepen at each stage. Meeting new people in two or three different settings can soon deepen the relationship. Deeper relationships equal increased caring, sharing and sense of family.

Practise hospitality and encourage others to do the same. Hospitality will be different in each context. With young people, it's often accepting them just as they are, listening to them and giving them quality time. It may be serving coffee and cake in a cafe setting, or setting up a crèche in an all-age setting.

Create a sense of purpose. Yes, the team might already have it, but new people need to pick up what we're all aiming to do together and the direction the group is heading in. People respond to vision, and this can create teamwork, offers of help and a sense that we're all heading on an adventure together.

Get new people involved without putting them off. As well as asking them to serve and help out, ask them what ideas they have about the group and how it can be made better. Really listen to their ideas and involve them in planning and running the group where appropriate.

Key questions

- What is your vision of community? What's the purpose?
- Who can you start to train and model this purpose with?
- How can you influence new people and involve them?
- How can you practise hospitality?
- How can new people get the vision and take ownership?

Community into Christian community – how do we get there?

First, go through a process of creating community (as above) as this builds trust, gives people a new family and a safe space. It also means people are more likely to trust and become open to listen to the community founders. People in Sorted usually find a sense of family before they find a faith in God, so community becomes a big part of the good news to new people. Building a community usually has to happen before it can become a Christian community, although in real life these distinctions can get blurred and might even occur in a different order. The journey on the ground can become messy.

Second, pray for the new people in your community and be creative in how you tell the good news (see 'Ways to be intentional when doing evangelism' above p. 90]). The stages of a fresh expression give us a way of providing just the right amount of Christian input for people in different stages of the fresh expression. Those who haven't been to church will need the gospel in short bursts as it will be new to them. By the way, don't wait for the community to form; share the gospel early on so it becomes part of the DNA of the new community.

Third, form a small group for those who are open to God and interested in exploring faith. In Sorted, forming community and forming faith go hand in hand − we run small groups for those open to God and those getting most into the community side of Sorted.

Fourth, just as you would listen and involve new people in forming community, so it's vital to listen and involve new people in hearing the gospel. Start an ongoing conversation so that you are on a spiritual journey together. Yes, the pioneer has to lead but, he or she should do it with both ears open and keep the approach flexible to how people are responding.

Fifth, contextualize the good news. With young people into heavy metal music, a discussion started around song lyrics that refer to heaven and hell. This led to conversation about what Jesus said about heaven and hell. A really good discussion ended up with a young person asking God into his life! Try writing a question for discussion that fits your context.

Sixth, make sure there is plenty of variety on the spiritual menu. Our POD short talks were often testimony- or short-story-based but we sometimes allow small group discussions to go off the planned subject. It's better to create a safe space for people to ask questions, explore openly and voice an opinion.

We encourage people to pray in the small group. James invented a way of praying where one person starts with a phrase, then others keep adding a phrase until it finishes. This worked well with people who speak informal phrases in their daily life rather than polished sentences, as many normal prayers become. The worship service experimented with sacred space, prayer tents, waiting on the Lord, and everything done with lots of interaction. Lots of variety helps different people connect with God.

Questions

- Who have you built relationships with? How might you introduce the Christian faith in bite-sized chunks?
- Are there people you can involve in setting up a small quiet time to pray or be silent with candles?
- Are there people showing interest in God? Is it possible to form a small group with such people to discuss Christian faith and/or spirituality?
- Do you know one or two people who could join you in thinking of creative ways to contextualize the Christian faith for your community and offer a varied spiritual menu?

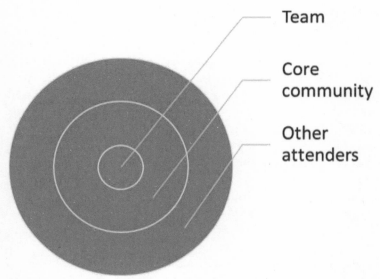

Team

Core community

Other attenders

Figure 4: A centred-set community

Can Christian community be 'rippled out' for others to join?

Figure 4, of a centred-set community, shows how people can move freely from the outside edge of a community towards its centre without the strict boundaries of a bounded-set community.

Michael Frost and Alan Hirsch distinguish 'centred-set' communities from 'bounded-set' communities.[7] Centred-set communities are defined by their core values. People are not in or out but closer or further from the centre. The 'stages' approach to a new church provides a natural pattern for people to be as close to the centre as they want. The stages approach should make it easier to both join a new church and go deeper into the community.

To make this work in practice, it's important to hold three things in tandem:

1   Core – develop a core of key people who share and model the vision and values. Evangelists like me can become so focused on helping new people to join, but if the core isn't nurtured, cared for and fed spiritually they can become disillusioned and eventually disintegrate.

2   Transitioning between stages – suppose there is a cafe where new people arrive, a small group to explore faith and a quiet worship space held weekly in a community facility. People need to be able to move from one to another. This works best if there are key people spread over more than one stage. If the key people build relationships across the stages, others will find it easier to naturally go with a key person into the next stage. For example, if there are two key people in both cafe and small group, others in the cafe have someone both to be a guide and to travel with into the small group.

3   New people – see below.

During a 2007 review of Sorted, Steve Hollinghurst observed how Sorted 1 is a distinct community that has flowed out of

THE DNA OF PIONEER MINISTRY

another community – Immanuel College. As we did detached work in Immanuel, we formed Sorted with a small nucleus of Immanuel students. From then on, new people would arrive at Sorted and settle in quickly because there were people at Sorted they recognized from Immanuel. Seeing their peers engage with Christianity was easier for them to embrace than if they had entered a community full of strangers engaging with Christianity. Arriving at Sorted for the first time, but then seeing their peers from Immanuel getting involved, somehow broke down social barriers and put new people at ease.

Are there existing communities that you could join so that a natural flow might develop from that community into the new church? Moynagh demonstrates how most New Testament churches met in homes and were gathered people, often from existing communities of different workers.[8] If new people gather from existing communities then it's often easier for them to share community life, learn about Christian faith and discover discipleship that makes sense in their specific context.

Handling a community in conflict

Last night's session had been a disaster! Bob the youth worker explained how the young people were falling out with each other and the two adults. Some were threatening to boycott the group. What had gone wrong?

There was disagreement over how long the introductory talk lasted. It had been getting longer each week. Bob and Jim forgot to develop a community and had reverted back to a situation where they were setting the agenda and everyone else had to follow. The core of the community felt marginalized and it was changing from a community into a crowd.

As we chatted, I asked Bob to remind me of the initial vision and which young people were founding members of the group. We came up with a plan. Bob would have one-to-one conversations with each founding member and a couple of other key people in the group. The conversation would include listening to each person's concerns and ideas while gently reminding them of the initial vision.

A few days later, the conversations went well. As it would turn out, they reminded Bob of the initial vision. Bob then arranged to meet these members together for a few minutes before each session so that he could involve them in running the session. The idea was to reignite the core of the community by getting everyone back to the initial vision.

Next week came. Bob arrived at the session with the wider group of young people. With the core starting to reignite, he reminded people of the vision, acknowledged there had been failures and asked the young people to join him in creating a session plan and ground rules for the group. Everyone got to voice their opinion. A plan and set of ground rules were soon agreed.

They allocated 15 minutes for the introductory talk. To prevent future conflict, I suggested a trusted young person should use a stopwatch and call time on the leader after 15 minutes. It needed a concrete action like this to keep the leaders to 15 minutes (Jim could go on for 30 minutes!) if the young people were going to trust the leaders and stick with the agreement.

Tips to solving disagreements

1 Remind everyone of the original vision in a sentence.
2 Everyone listens to someone's proposition – complaint, idea, etc.
3 Discuss the question: do we agree with this in principle?
4 If so, have we any practical ideas to make it better?

Another common problem when forming a new community is how to integrate people who wouldn't normally mix together. It may simply be a case of letting new people get used to each other. This can take a year or two, but sometimes there can be prejudice between groups that keeps them apart. We found this as young people from different teen tribes, such as skaters and townies, just wouldn't mix. Differences in dress, fashion, music and friendship groups kept them apart.

Forming a community with adults from a middle-class area and from a council estate might be problematic, as could adults with differences in age, gender, race or subculture. They might love mixing with different adults but equally they might simply find it hard to integrate. How do you form community with groups that naturally find it hard to integrate?

Once again, the stages approach can help solve this problem. As new people from different teen tribes became interested in God and more involved in Sorted, they joined our mini community. As time went by, finding both an identity in Sorted and a common purpose through being involved, they started relating to each other as people sharing a common purpose. As these same people became Christians and experienced the Holy Spirit, the differences melted away and became irrelevant. Adults moving into a deeper 'stage' of a new church may discover a shared sense of purpose with people from totally different backgrounds.

Sanctus 1 – by Ben Edson[9]

'We have moved from a Cathedral to a parish church and now moved again to an arts café. We have seen the community grow from four to fifty; then from fifty to twenty and currently from twenty back to fifty. We have experimented with mid-week groups, small groups, groups on Sundays and no groups. We have been involved in running club nights, in mind body spirit fayres, in art exhibitions and a night café. Change is part of our story.

Each new person that comes to Sanctus1 changes the community; their unique presence brings a new dynamic, a new set of experiences and new areas of wisdom. This "openness to the wisdom of the new" means that the old is permanently being refreshed . . .

The values need to remain provisional so that each person who comes to Sanctus1 feels that they can influence them so that they reflect the current community . . . Within this culture of provisionality the story-tellers and the story-carriers become very important as people who carry the narrative of Sanctus1 with them so that when the future is planned it remains consistent with the story of the past. It is often the case that the leader of a community becomes the central story-teller, however a less dependent and more sustainable way is for the community to become a story-telling community.

When a community shares and lives the story they then will go on to write the story, to start a new sentence and dream the next chapter. This has happened within Sanctus1 by the leadership being shared between a team of up to five people, with that team being a mix of clergy and laity, male and female. This team aims to be fluid, enabling people to commit to it for an appropriate time-period rather than indefinitely. The story-tellers of Sanctus1 are then not only the leadership team but everyone involved in living the story of the community and serving the city centre of Manchester.'

Ben gets to the heart of what it means to form Christian community — every person brings something unique that makes the community what it is, each member is to own the story of the community and be part of writing its future, the community is fluid because it's the living Body of Christ. Whatever the community, every member matters!

Notes

1 Simon and Val Thomas got involved as volunteers and gave 100% right from day one of Sorted. They became good friends with Tracy and me, and we often went off in our caravans together during holiday time. The four of us became the backbone of Sorted

in the early years. (Val is now our Reader and began Thrive, while Simon is one of the church wardens.)

2 Church Army's *Stepping into Evangelism* booklet is a great, up-to-date resource with lots of helpful ways to do evangelism: http://www.churcharmy.org.uk/Groups/244431/Church_Army/Church _Army/Resources/Stepping_into_evangelism/Stepping_into.aspx.

3 Michael Moynagh, *Church for Every Context*, London: SCM Press, 2012, p. 334.

4 'The Living Room and Franky's Pizza' story by Tina Powsey: http://www.freshexpressions.org.uk/stories/livingroom-frankyspizza/nov15.

5 Moynagh, *Church for Every Context*, p. 380.

6 Not all pioneers will need to do this; the pioneering team might be able to model community effectively simply by inviting the new people into a new group consisting of the team and new people together. This is more likely with some adult groups or some all-age settings.

7 Michael Frost and Alan Hirsch, *The Shape of Things to Come: Innovation and Mission for the 21st-Century Church*, Peabody, MA: Hendrickson, 2003, pp. 47–51.

8 Moynagh, *Church for Every Context*, p. 6.

9 Story by Ben Edson: http://www.freshexpressions.org.uk/stories /sanctus1.

7

What's so good about small groups, and how do I make disciples?

If only it were that simple ...

Pioneers need to keep asking one simple question – How do we get people interested in a passionate relationship with Jesus? In other words, how do we get people to become Christians and grow as mature disciples? We will need to create non-threatening spaces where relationships with new people can develop and ongoing conversations about Jesus can happen.

Small groups are ideal environments for this to take place. If small groups are done well, they are like nutrient-rich bags of soil, perfect for planting seeds of faith. Trust will spread, conversations about Jesus will arise and conversions happen if the soil is good. So how do we create good soil?

There are loads of courses for small discussion groups, such as Alpha, Emmaus or Start, and there is much published teaching material that can be used in small groups. But pioneers need to keep asking – What will work in our context? Do we buy the course material, do we create our own group discussion material, or mix and match? What will work with the group of people I'm currently working with?

This chapter starts by looking at how a small group developed in Sorted. We explore some of its successes and failures so that we might gain insights into what ingredients make good soil for a small group to flourish. Second, the chapter goes on to tell a story of how someone became a disciple within Sorted, looking beyond the small group to the broader picture of how we make disciples through relationships, different groups, different contexts and by being involved in mission.

Setting up small groups in Sorted

As I thought about some of these questions, part of the answer came from reading in Mike Breen's *Outside In*,[1] how Jesus' followers were sent to look for people of peace in Matthew 10, Mark 6 and Luke 10. As I would soon discover, youngsters who were people of peace would become the bridges or connection points between me and their friends. As I formed a small group with a young person of peace, they in turn became a crucial factor in determining which other youngsters would attend. The level of openness within the group was often dependent on these one or two people. People of peace help to create good soil.

During one lunch break, as I was walking round the playground at Immanuel College (the secondary school where the detached work was happening) in summer 2004, I got chatting to Ben, who was 13 and already had a faith in God. He was committed to his faith and yet it was very much a thing that happened on Sundays in his church. Ben had lots of friends who were ordinary young people (quite a few with little or no faith) living in the area. I suggested that we should start meeting up on Wednesdays after school to skate and chat; he should bring some of his mates and I would bring Robert from the Sorted team.

Although six young people came out to meet us and have a skate on the first day, the 'Wednesday group' would typically consist of Ben, me, Robert and sometimes James. We all got on well; the two lads were open and happy to discuss God, but where were their mates? After eight or nine months of trying to run a group with only one or sometimes two young people, I started to think about quitting this group and trying something else. As I prayed, I had a sense of God saying, 'Keep going with it', so we did.

During the summer of 2005 (just as the POD was starting to attract 20 or more young people) we set up another small group. Yet again, Ben was the person of peace. We decided to try and meet on an evening because we thought more of Ben's mates would be available to come along. So one Tuesday night, Ben and two of his mates joined up with me and Richard (from the Sorted team). We met in Ben's house almost every Tuesday for the next 15 months.

Experimenting . . .

The first Tuesday night came and we met together. Although I knew Ben well, I didn't know his mates very well and they didn't know Richard at all. Nevertheless, I asked everyone to sit and decide together what we were going to do each Tuesday and how we would make it happen.

I took a facilitative approach, trying to get the young people to feel confident enough to speak their minds and be honest if they were not happy with the direction we were heading. I often find with new groups of non-churched youngsters that it's crucial I hold myself back but keep the group focused, taking a gentle approach so that the young people feel emboldened not only to speak but to take ownership too. This approach also allows young people to feel that we are all in this together, and usually strengthens relationships.

As it happened, we really did come to a joint decision. After I threw in a suggestion, they discussed it and then Ben said, 'Why don't we spend half the time chatting (about God or a life issue) and the other half of the time chilling on the computer game or skateboarding.' Everyone agreed, and so 'chill and chat' became the formula for Tuesday nights. As the weeks went by, I would bring the discussion topic and the young people would decide how we were going to 'chill', often choosing to stay in Ben's house gaming or going out to skate. It was important that they decided the chill bit and this became a tangible weekly expression of their ownership of the group.

From then on, the group grew at a steady pace as Ben and others invited their friends. A typical night would consist of a 20-minute discussion (in practice, 50% of the night chatting was too much for them and had to be reduced), using the Bible and praying together. Many of the young people came to believe, pray and start their own journey of faith.

Sometimes young people didn't want to do the discussion but the people of peace (Ben and now James), with their positive enthusiasm, ensured that it would happen and at the same time became infectious and brought on the enthusiasm of the others. Ben and James were much more effective at motivating their peers than I could be.

Skateboarding, gaming or playing piggy in the middle with a football became a great opportunity to grab brief one-to-one chats with the young people without the others listening. This was the time when they started to talk to me about their problems, or, if something from a discussion had touched a nerve, they would tell me in between landing skate tricks or waiting for a go on the games console. I came to realize that the 'chill' time really complemented the 'chat' time and both were crucial for faith-building and relationship-building.

Building a good relationship with Ben and James was important simply because of their influence on the others as people of peace. The effects of James' difficult family life would come out in different ways at different times. For example, he would often react badly to any kind of competitive game that didn't go his way, including a skateboarding game called Skate. One winter evening, the group were using the grounds of a local school. James, Ben and I were playing Skate using skateboards on the tarmac. I could tell that things were about to go wrong with James. So for my next trick, I skated up to the steps as if to do a trick and simply dived off the board and rolled on to the cold, wet grass. They both laughed and the game stopped as we started having fun doing dafter and dafter things on skateboards. It took the sting out of the situation, created a few laughs and showed the two lads that I was not above being daft and having fun with them.

Andy with Sorted skaters in 2005, including a young Carl Firth (top far right) who is now a youth worker with Sorted.

Andy explaining the Bible at a Friday night session in 2006.

Tracy giving the young people a first taster of worship at a Friday night session in 2006.

A young person getting baptized in the river by Bishop David James in 2010 – a key supporter of Sorted until he retired.

Carl and Lynzi came to Sorted as young people and eventually got married!!! Carl is our youth worker and Lynzi is now one of the church wardens (2014).

James Hawksworth baptizing a young person in 2012.

Sorted1 in 2013.

Summer camp 2011 with long standing team members Simon and Val Thomas (stood together on the right at the end) and Nick Lebey who later would take the Sorted model to London and begin TYM, a fresh expression among young people (next to me on the far left).

Getting into God's book on camp in 2012.

Praying for one another in 2015.

'If you don't obey the rules …' Lol. Guys from Sorted having fun while making a film about Jesus in 2011.

Young people worship at Tracy's licensing service in 2016.

Actually, most Sorted pictures are like this one, young people in 2012 simply having fun.

Worshipping in 2015.

Young people on a Friday night in 2016.

Sorted 3 in 2015 including Damien Hine (centre adult).

How do we build on this one successful experiment?

By the start of 2006, there were six regular young people at the Tuesday-night group. Although it was still early days, it did seem like we were on to something and here was an opportunity to build on.

So how did a typical discussion work? After several failed attempts at getting the process right, we came upon a successful routine. After first asking everyone to sit in a circle, I would go round the group, asking everyone to share whether they'd had a good or bad week and why. This showed care and concern, while getting the members of the group to open up a little. Another group might use an ice-breaker such as a fun game or fun exercise just to loosen everyone up. There are so many books of ice-breakers and they work well with people of any age.

After an opening prayer, everyone would take a youth Bible. A young person would be asked to read the chosen passage and then we might have three or four simple questions aimed at getting a discussion going. These were always open questions designed to maximize conversation. The first question would be very simple and aimed to provoke a response from everyone. The middle questions usually focused on the topic, while the last question would challenge us to do something about what we had learnt.

Quite often the discussions would go off the planned subject but were valuable anyway. Sometimes I let the discussions drift off track if they were productive, not wanting to dampen the enthusiasm. I would plan to throw in a couple of true stories that showed how someone had encountered God. These stories could be used or not used depending on which direction the discussion were to take. As it happened, at least one story was usually told and these stories became a crucial part of the discussion. I quickly discovered that allowing the discussion to wander was vital; it was nearly always better to go where the youngsters wanted to go and link it to God rather than force them to stick to the topic and lose interest.

Other groups might discuss a DVD clip, song lyrics, a latest news item or whatever. Creating discussion about faith and God is the aim. The Bible is obviously an easy way in but some groups aren't ready to begin with the Bible. So start where they are at.

We sometimes had to use different rooms in Ben's house. The living room, full of comfortable chairs already in a circle, helped the group to function well. I was starting to discover just how important the setting is for a discussion group.

Comfortable seating, few distractions, warmth, chairs set out in a circle and Bibles already placed on the chairs (if the group is in the habit of using the Bible, but not for the first two or three meetings with some non-churched youngsters) can really help make the group work well. Too much space can be unhelpful; too little space can also be a hindrance. Snack food and drinks at the start or in the middle of the session can also help people settle.

Some factors to consider when starting a small group

Is there a person of peace?

If evangelism is defined as 'seeing what God is doing in mission and joining in',[2] then a person of peace should be defined as 'the most obvious place to begin looking for what God is doing in mission'. People of peace are important because ultimately churches are pioneered through relationships, and a person of peace is open to building a relationship with God and the pioneer.

People of peace become bridges or positive influences to others so that lots of people can be reached through them. Without them, it might be much harder to connect with these other people. This happened with Ben, but also happened when Jesus met the Samaritan woman at the well (John 4) and when Paul met Lydia (Acts 16). Jesus clearly knew how important the woman at the well would be (he sent off the 12 disciples to buy lunch for 13 to get them out of the way) when he prophesied to her about her life. After she opened up to Jesus, she was soon off to tell her village about him. She became a bridge to her village so that Jesus could connect with her people, who would go on to put their faith in him.

This is question to ask God – who are the people of peace? How can I build a relationship with such a person or people? With Ben, I simply kept chatting to him in school until it became obvious that we could form a group.

People of peace can teach us about the culture of their group and about its members. Ben would sometimes act as an interpreter, helping me figure out what discussion subjects would be relevant because he knew the group members better than me. He would also communicate back to me the problems that others weren't telling me; that is, if they were unhappy about an aspect of the group or if someone was going through a tough situation at home. Ben did this sensitively so as not to break confidences, but it really helped me to get a feel for the group in the first few months.

Build relationally

As our Tuesday group grew, it was like laying bricks of a similar size and shape that fitted together naturally. Friends brought friends and this cemented the group together. We did have a few others come and go but those who came and already knew the existing members tended to stay. I'm convinced this principle holds in most contexts; it's much harder to build a sustainable group over a period of time by bringing together complete strangers. Building relationally tends to cement the group together quicker, establish trust quicker and increase the chances of the group staying together.

'People of peace' and 'building relationally' are complementary parts of God's mission strategy. Jesus said, 'seek people of peace . . . stay with them' (Luke 10). Jesus wants us to find people of peace (so we see who God is already working in) and stay with them so that, like the Samaritan woman, they will help connect us with their circle of friends, family or work colleagues. New people will be added to our small group from within these circles.

Encourage openness

As the Tuesday group started, I had to balance trying to listen to the Spirit with involving the young people in coming up with ideas and making decisions. The 'chill and chat' approach provided a good way to do this. I would prayerfully plan the 'chat' discussion topic, whereas the 'chill' space opened a natural weekly opportunity for the group to discuss and choose what activities they wanted to do during the second half of the night. This was a good way to open things up and give the group ownership of this part of the session. Ownership is important, but so is openness. By trying to open up conversation and encourage everyone to speak, group members would open up and share ideas and opinions about God and this would provoke more conversations about faith, not fewer.

Be pastoral

As I said in the story above, the recreation time brought lots of opportunities for one-to-one pastoral conversations. These conversations led to discussion of how God might bring help in the tough, painful circumstances of a person's life. As trust was built over time, barriers to faith gradually shrank. Many people come to faith when their life hits a crisis and so it is important to help people recognize how God wants to comfort, strengthen and support them in their day-to-day lives.

Be practical

A good, well-planned environment can really help a small group function well. Warmth, comfort, lighting, music, food and drink all done well can remove distractions and create a cosy, welcoming and attractive environment. At Sorted, we've had groups in both good and bad environments. There is no doubt in my mind as to which one works! A good environment can't guarantee a group will be successful but it might give it the boost it needs. A bad environment can kill an otherwise good group.

Travel the learning loop

A group is like a young family; it will need lots of care and attention in the right areas at the right time. So ask group members for their feedback on how they think the group is functioning, ask the people of peace and reflect by asking questions (see Figure 5).

Travel round the learning loop with others so that it becomes normal to reflect on what is happening; pray, discuss and then plan ahead based on what you are learning. You are then more likely to develop a culture of learning that helps to solve problems and build on successes.

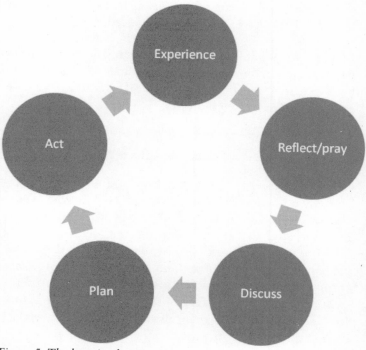

Figure 5: The learning loop

Keep the vision

What has God called you to do with this group or what does God want to do through this group? If at any point you become unsure, spend some time praying about this, perhaps reflecting on some key Bible passages:

Matthew 28.19 – The great commission tells us it's all about making disciples. Is the group moving people in the direction of making disciples? If not, why not? What is hindering the process? Can hindrances be removed or reduced? If disciple-making is happening, what is helping the process? How can we encourage this more?

Matthew 16.18 – Jesus promises to build his church, so is Christian community being built? Once again, it's good to ask questions of whether this is happening. If so, why and how can we collaborate with Jesus as he builds his church? If it's not happening, does something need changing?

Ezekiel 34 – What kind of leadership do you model? In this passage, God outlines some of the qualities of a caring 'shepherd' leader. Read and ask God to give you these qualities and to help grow them in others.

Essence – by the Revd James Blandford-Baker[3]

'When Essence was launched, we prayed for five people to show up on the first Wednesday and ten arrived. The format worked from the outset; people talked naturally and honestly, sharing their stories and engaging fully with the Christian story. By week three, people were exchanging mobile phone numbers; community was forming. Not long afterwards people began to look after each other when they were in need. It is quite normal for a new mother to have meals for the family delivered each evening for a fortnight.'

By telling some of the story of Essence, James sums up the nitty-gritty of why small groups are important – chatting, sharing and listening to each other's stories, becoming friends and serving one another.

Exploring discipleship

I've heard Christians say, 'If only we could get people beyond head knowledge into heartfelt discipleship, then my church would be transformed!' When beginning Sorted, I was tempted to think, 'It would just be nice to have a Christian or two coming through!' Getting people to become heartfelt disciples of Jesus seemed a long way off.

Much of the approach to making disciples has focused on imparting knowledge[4] to new members or gaining qualifications for those training for professional ministry. Yet the gist of discipleship in the Gospels is about being with Jesus, seeing how he does things and learning from him, like an apprentice joiner learns from an experienced joiner. Our approach can seem tilted towards gaining head knowledge, yet Jesus' approach was to make disciples in the hustle and bustle of life. His approach led to life transformation as his followers learnt from him with others in community.

If the task of making disciples seems daunting, then I hope this chapter gives you a new way of looking at things. Pioneers start with a blank sheet of paper, giving us the opportunity for fresh thinking and experimenting. When a man and a woman make love, the miraculous birthing of a child may be set in motion. One of the wonderful things about a new child is spotting the many ways in which the baby looks like mum and dad. This can only happen because of the amazing way our DNA influences the 'make-up' of our children.

As God uses us to birth a new church, the DNA of the pioneers will influence how the blank canvas is painted upon. Although we'll learn lots as we go, just as a parent learns by bringing up a child, our initial DNA (thinking, leading and ways of working) has a big influence on how things develop. When it comes to the DNA needed to make disciples, this leaves questions. Have we got it? If not, where can we get it from? How can we inject disciple-making DNA into the pioneering process at the beginning of a new church? Pioneering something totally new gives God the opportunity to do something amazing among us, yet it will take time and persistence.

With a baby, all parents want a successful birth, but no parent in their right mind would only be satisfied to stop there; they all want their baby to grow into a mature person. Shouldn't we want the same thing for baby Christians? Disciple-making includes both bringing people to faith and enabling them to grow into mature discipleship. Sometimes these two processes overlap and are hard to distinguish between, as we see in the story below.

Billy

I met Billy in the school canteen when he was 11. We got on well and Billy soon started attending our Friday-night POD session. Billy started asking me questions about my 'God talks', listening intently as I explained how God had worked in my life.

As Tracy and I got to know Billy, we discovered his family life wasn't great – divorced parents, a dad who favoured his brother over him, and a loving mum, yet in the process of overcoming alcohol addiction while bringing up two teenage boys on her own! Tracy suggested we invite Billy for tea on a night when his mum wouldn't be home till late so he wouldn't have to cook for himself. This soon became a weekly thing as we tried to provide a bit of support for Billy.

Billy then came to a small group. His openness to God grew and we had many conversations about faith. As Billy moved through the stages of Sorted – Friday POD, small group and then worship service – he also moved closer to God, becoming a Christian and starting a journey of discipleship.

'This place is keeping you away from Satan!' said his new girlfriend as she tried to pull Billy out of our worship service. Billy felt scared (wouldn't you?) and torn between her and us. Deep down, he knew this girl was on the wrong track and that God was real, so he decided to stop dating her. There had been a weird atmosphere in the church when the girl and her friends had entered; the peaceful presence of God seemed to evaporate and it really felt like a spiritual battle. Thankfully, some of those into Satanism switched sides soon after and chose Jesus.

Around this time, Billy first came with us to Soul Survivor. Along with other young people, I took Billy to visit churches, interviewing him so he could tell how he had recently come to faith. Both these experiences introduced Billy to the wider Church so that when he was baptized by the Bishop, he began to understand that he was part of a worldwide Church.

'I read some [Bible] just like Billy does', said his mate Rob as he told me how he had been at Billy's house, seen the Youth Bible and Billy had shown him how to read it (devotionally).

'Was it real?' asked Sam on another occasion. Billy was being asked by his mate Sam whether or not his recent spiritual experience at Sorted was real or imagined. Billy now had a reputation of both having God in his life and yet still being someone the tough, school-excluded lads could relate to.

Over the next year, Billy and another mate set up a small prayer tent at our worship service and led a Bible discussion group. Billy now aspired to become a youth worker. Discipleship was happening in Billy's life on all sorts of levels:

- community member (through our family, one-to-one conversations and in Sorted)
- faith in Jesus (evidenced by prayer, Bible reading, prayer tent and change in character)
- mission – telling his peers about his faith (see conversations above)
- serving (leading groups)
- exposure to the wider Church (Soul Survivor festival and other churches).

In some ways, it was 'total discipleship'! Billy had both become a Christian and begun the process of growing into maturity – it would be a long road but he had started the journey.

Big picture

To inject disciple-making DNA from day one, we need to have an idea of which direction to head in. Here are four things to consider when looking at the big picture of making disciples.

1 How does the mission context influence disciple-making?

In our increasingly postmodern world, commitment comes slowly.[5] Many grow up into a personalized world where we choose what to buy and often develop our identity around what we buy. Discipleship requires commitment, dying to self and learning to let Jesus live in us. Much of our culture clashes with discipleship. Yet in the mess of broken relationships and dissatisfaction with the 'me' culture, people are searching for authentic relationships and to belong to a family or community. The recent big growth in fresh expressions of church is proof that people want such families. Forming new Christian communities will provide opportunities for people to find Jesus and become disciples. Belonging to the Sorted family played a pivotal role in Billy's discipleship.

Mike Moynagh explains how disciple-making has shifted from a point of conversion (prayer of commitment), to a process in the 1990s (often via a Christian basics course), to a quest (individual journey to discipleship).[6] This reflects the journeys many people are likely to travel to become a committed disciple of Jesus. Processes and points can still be important parts of the quest, just as some people use pictures to show important points of their life on their Facebook timeline, but it's less likely these points or processes on their own will equal discipleship.

Also, it's likely to take longer than it used to because people increasingly travel towards God with no previous church experience. Each journey will be different, yet long-term authentic relationships with influential Christians and learning within a community are vital. This means that our approach to disciple-making should aim both to bring people to faith and to grow them into maturity. As with Billy, it's likely these processes will overlap as people develop discipleship habits before, during and after conversion. For example, some of our young people learnt to give financially before praying a prayer of commitment.

2 Begin with the end in mind

When we began Sorted, someone asked me, 'What do you want? Is it enough for you to see one or two people become Christians? Or (taking it further), is it enough for you to have Christians who are learning to become disciples? Or (taking it further), is it enough to have some disciples who are becoming lay leaders? Or (taking it further), do you want to make disciples, some of whom will go on to become ministers or evangelists?' I was blown over by these questions! I thought about them a lot. I could feel pressurized by them or pray for ways to make disciples – some of whom might even become ministers. But Jesus says 'make disciples', he doesn't say only pray for them or leave the responsibility of being a disciple totally with the new Christian. So how do we even begin to think about a process of making disciples, some of whom might become ministers?

These questions above give us some clues. They suggest that different things are needed to make Christians/disciples/lay leaders or ministers. We need to be intentional, while taking things one step at a time. Some parents know they eventually want three or four children, yet during the first pregnancy they can't possibly get their heads round the third or fourth child, they just need to focus on one (just ask the mum!). A student wanting to become a doctor will know this requires A levels, university and the study of medicine, but at age 15, she can only focus on her GCSEs. We should begin with the end in mind, keeping one eye on the big picture while focusing on the one thing we are developing at that moment.

3 Beginning to develop a 'customized method' of disciple-making that will work with your people

As the new church develops, it's important to keeping asking, 'How does this help these people come to faith and become disciples?' Many Christian basics courses such as Alpha, Emmaus or Start were developed in specific contexts. Don't just assume that using such a course automatically helps people to become disciples in your context. It's better to pick out what will suit your people from various courses and customize your approach to fit the context. For example, Alpha was too long and information heavy for our guys, so we picked out key parts of the talks, practised the 'Holy Spirit ministry' times and put more emphasis on involving everyone in running the session together and learning to live out Christian values like forgiveness within our community. All these courses have hidden gems, so don't be afraid to pick them out! Be creative, cut and paste and listen and observe how your people engage or struggle with parts of a course so that you can adapt better.

4 See what God is doing and join in

If we decide to try and make disciples, God will be at work with us. Like Philippians 2.12, we have to work out our salvation (or disciple-making), yet God is at work within the process. Rick Warren comments that pioneering a church is like learning to surf waves of the Spirit that God is sending our way.[7] Our job is to see the waves he's sending and learn to surf them.

A few months after starting our POD session, I was impatient to invite more people to it. I sensed God nudging me to start thinking about a small group so that those most open to God could explore Christian faith. This would turn out to be a another step on the road into discipleship for some young people. Jesus said, 'I will build my church' (Matthew 16.18), and so God is always wanting to form, grow and deepen his community and add new dimensions to our community life.

When sensing God may be sending a new spiritual wave, it can be easy to miss by not seeing it or to dismiss it because it doesn't immediately fit our current understanding. John Wimber would take an A4 writing pad and spend some time noting all the things that were pointing towards the new thing that God is doing.[8] For example, if God wants you to begin a small group, you might expect to see two or more people hungry for it or asking for a space to chat about God or Christian faith. Sometimes it will be obvious, but at other times we might need to search a bit harder. Praying and chatting with others can help us discern what God is doing.

Being intentional

DNA

Our plan for making disciples was simply to persist in prayer, keep nudging people deeper into God and create opportunities for this to happen. We had to be flexible, learn slowly from our mistakes and keep trying. I think this is what it means to be intentional.

It is unlikely disciples will be made from among those far away from church and with little or no Christian background by simply starting a new course on discipleship. In reality, you're going to have to:

- create a community where people see discipleship lived out (whether or not they know what it is)
- create spaces where people can find Jesus and be exposed to ongoing teaching/prayer/worship
- create opportunities to put discipleship into practice
- nurture those who are becoming disciples through deep relationships.

Tools

You might read the above and think, 'That's OK, but how does this happen in practice, especially when discipleship needs to be customized to context?'

I imagine it as having a set of tools for making disciples in a tool bag but, until you arrive on the job, you simply don't know when different tools will be needed. So I imagined that Sorted would need some sort of small group so that people could discuss, ask questions, engage in conversation, but also experiment by reading the Bible, praying and helping others. My gut feeling was that these things would happen best in a small group, but I didn't know when the people would be ready for such a group. The worship service is another example of a tool in the bag. My guess was that we'd need one for deeper teaching, worship and deeper prayer, but I had to be content with this being a tool in my bag that would only be used when God was nudging us and we could see that the time was right for some of our people to engage in this.

Being intentional means thinking ahead and prayerfully pondering, 'What tools are going to be needed and how might they be used effectively to enable discipleship?' But don't take the tools out of the bag until the people are ready; plan ahead, but be patient until it's the right time. Use one tool at a time; develop it until it works well before starting on the next tool.

Ingredients

Billy's story shows that a variety of ingredients are needed to make a disciple. Moynagh highlights several ingredients that can really aid the discipleship process:[9]

1 *Acts of kindness* that reveal compassion; for example, Billy coming round for tea each week.
2 *God-talk* – little and often at events and in conversations; for example, sparked conversations with Billy.
3 *Missional worship* – encountering God, seeing others worship authentically, provokes a search for the spiritual; for example,

our worship service created an environment where Billy and his peers encountered God.

4 *Answered prayer* – including healing or help to discern how God is at work.

5 *Creative expressions of spirituality* might involve the new people in being creative; for example, Billy's involvement in the prayer tent.

If the DNA is the first layer of the cake, the tools provide the second layer and the ingredients are the icing on top. One problem of the church being over-focused on imparting knowledge in discipleship is that it can become dry, irrelevant or off-putting for those who didn't enjoy school. Encountering God through an answered prayer, a talk or an act of kindness is a sign of the kingdom breaking in; it's potentially putting people in connection with God for the first time; it's seeing what we say lived out in reality.

The ingredients above are simply what happens when God is central to our disciple-making. Are we building God-talk into our gathering sessions and seeking it in conversation? Are we asking God to give us opportunities to pray with people for their needs? People with little church experience need to hear about God in a relevant way fairly often for their interest to be aroused. Otherwise, if they've gone through life not really thinking about him, why start now unless they are exposed to interesting and relevant God-talk in bite-sized pieces?

Culture

There are various approaches to the interface of Christianity and culture. The challenge is to both affirm those parts of the culture that conform to Christian values and find ways to reform, challenge or provide alternatives to those parts of culture that oppose Christian values. Tolerance for other religions and lifestyles is big today and it's important that we really love and accept people, demonstrating kindness and patience without judging. With young people who are being challenged by their school or parents, we found that demonstrating unconditional love and acceptance would have a big impact with many, making it possible for trust and healthy relationships to develop.

With cultural traits that oppose Christian values, we've tried to take different approaches. When trying to get young people away from being consumers of Sorted, we find key young people who want to get involved and serve and then build little teams of young people who model taking ownership and sharing responsibility. These young people quietly challenge consumerism by their actions and reform their culture. With a young person struggling with sexuality or a young person of another faith, we would go the extra mile to show we accept and love them as people, being careful not to judge. These young people will often expect us to judge them because of what they've heard in the media about Christians. If one of these young people comes to faith or if our relationship deepens so that there is genuine trust, this might lead to exploration using the Bible (or a trusted Christian book) with the young person and prayer over their sexuality or faith. I once sought support from True Freedom Trust[10] on a sexuality issue for a young person and I try to 'speak the truth in love' (Ephesians 4) and support the young person in whatever decisions they may take.

Stages

Bringing people to a decision 'point' at an evangelistic rally made sense when many or most in our country knew the Christian story, as it was a way to call people back to God or church. Taking people through a Christian basics course as a 'process' to bring about discipleship might make sense for those who've had experience of church. Creating a set of 'stages' to enable people to move into discipleship over a longer period of time makes sense in a country where a majority of people have never been to church beyond a wedding, funeral or baptism service. How do these 'stages' help us to make disciples?

With a set of stages, people can check in at a number of stages simultaneously or take one stage at a time. It's important that people hear the gospel and participate in the worshipping life of a church in a way they are ready for and will benefit from. Many of our young people attend our Friday session for a couple of years before they are ready to join a small group or attend a worship service. This allows them to hear a simple gospel message but not become overwhelmed by a sermon they don't understand. One of the reasons the Church has lost lots of people in recent decades is because we've expected people with little Christian knowledge or experience to join a worship service where they don't understand it, but we've also lost opportunities for Christian disciples to practise their faith in social outreach settings. Stages enable newcomers to add a stage (whether it be to join a small group or attend worship) at the pace of their discipleship, but also encourage those who've become worshippers to go back to the earlier stages (Friday-night social session or school lunch club) to serve as a team member as part of their discipleship in their context.

A key part of the discipleship process in Sorted is when new Christians join an outreach team, share a testimony or help with schools or pub work. The process of going out in mission, praying and caring for others, building relationships with new people and talking about the Christian faith really helps their formation as disciples. It's important that disciples are formed in the context of doing mission, which will accelerate their growth. A set of stages enables new Christians to be involved in doing mission via the earlier stages of a fresh expression. (For more on how this happened in Sorted, read the section on 'Worship and mission' in Chapter 8.)

Stages help the new church become contextual (Friday social session), formational (small group), ecclesial (worship service) and missional (as new people serve in teams in school or at the Friday social session), and this helps a new church take a total approach towards discipleship.[11]

Team discipleship checklist

As a team it's good to keep reviewing whether discipleship is happening by asking questions. Are people encountering God? Are people serving and starting to belong to the community? Are people engaging with prayer or Bible or talks at some level? Later on, are people becoming Christians and are their lives seeing transformation at some level? Because we're expecting people to travel on a quest, it's likely that things will happen gradually. Transformation might happen when someone becomes kinder or a person with anger issues gains patience, yet don't be discouraged if other areas of the person's life don't seem much transformed; that can come later. The important thing is the direction of travel people have started and keeping them moving, however slow it may seem.

Key Bible passages can keep a team focused: Rick Warren wants to see people fulfilling the great commission (Matthew 28 – make disciples) and the great commandments (love God, love people).[12] What key Bible passages have influenced you? Can these passages give the team clear aims and the inspiration and challenge to think how they are doing church?

Spiritual direction

Discipleship and spiritual direction happened for Billy a informal times. We would never have called it that but light conversation, looking at the Bible, discussion about life issues, encouragement and support, all rolled into one, equalled spiritual direction, as well as other times when we simply played games with Tracy and Sam.

Years later, one-to-one meetings with young people became a normal part of daily life for James, one of our team. Usually in a cafe, he would set short Bible readings for people to do between sessions, discuss prayer and help people connect their life issues to their walk with God. James would adapt his method for different individuals, sometimes spending a lot of time listening and helping people connect the dots in their life, challenging, encouraging or simply giving people space to be.

Having someone to journey with a new Christian one-to-one is important; we all need safe spaces to let off steam, work things out with objective support and be encouraged to keep getting to know God through tough times.

Interns, gap-year students or work-experience placements

It was impractical for Sorted to run a full gap-year programme for lots of reasons, yet we wanted to give people the opportunity to get more hands-on experience of serving both behind the scenes and preparing/running sessions, coupled with team meetings that would include quiet times, reflection and planning. We've seen quite a few people on a part-time gap-year or work-experience placement so that they can go further in their discipleship by being involved in the above.

Focused times such as part-time gap years can really help people develop new skills, discover a calling or go deeper with God by being more involved. Frequently, we find people amazed by how much goes on behind the scenes and the impact of continually being involved in a spiritual environment. People often take on roles during a gap year and continue those roles after the gap year has ended.

'Playthegame' training

If discipleship is enhanced through starting to serve, belonging, growing in faith and one-to-one spiritual direction, we also found that getting together a small number of emerging leaders for prayer and training can add value. Getting together the key emerging leaders gives opportunity for focused training on a relevant issue. Mixing up input, discussion, prayer and interactive learning keeps it real and relevant.

Crossnet – Bristol[13]

Nick Crawley writes: 'We disciple people with specific, focused, intentional mentoring . . . working out what faith means in your life and putting it into practice with the help of someone challenging you and helping you to do that is very rewarding . . . Following a community *Rule of life*, meeting in *Pods* (small groups with a Bible focus) and developing *Holy Habits* (practices that help shape our thoughts, feelings and actions in a way that allows us to engage with the transforming power of God to shape our lives to look like the life of Jesus) are some of the ways we encourage discipleship.'

George Lings writes: 'Some assume all fresh expressions of church can or should become large churches, even those that are network-focused. However over the years, Crossnet in Bristol have discovered remaining small can be a significant gift. Their story offers valuable insight into how apprentice-style models of discipleship done among the few are more effective than traditional methods of discipleship among the many. It is a good reminder that the wider church needs a mix of specific, highly intentional, flexible churches, more reminiscent of monastic groups, as well as parochial, generalist, settled churches.'[14]

Finally

Billy's story sums up what I've been trying to get across in this chapter. Discipleship involves a lot of things, such as eating with people, one-to-one chats, worship, mission and being exposed to the wider Church. Discipleship is likely to take a long time in our culture and the specifics probably need working out in each local situation. Yet meaningful relationship-building within a community is always going to be really important. Small groups are often the best places for meaningful relationships to develop and for people to explore faith at their own pace. Do consider setting up a small group or two as part of your disciple-making plan.

Notes

1 Mike Breen, *Outside In*, London: Scripture Union, 1993.
2 Raymond Fung, *The Isaiah Vision: Ecumenical Strategy for Congregational Evangelism*, Geneva: World Council of Churches, 1992.
3 Story by the Revd James Blandford-Baker: https://www.freshex pressions.org.uk/stories/essence.
4 Michael Moynagh, *Church for Every Context*, London: SCM Press, 2012, p. 338.
5 Moynagh, *Church for Every Context*, p. 341.
6 Moynagh, *Church for Every Context*, p. 338.
7 Rick Warren, *The Purpose Driven Church*, Grand Rapids, MI: Zondervan, 1995, p. 44.
8 John Wimber in *Cutting Edge Magazine* 7:7.
9 Moynagh, *Church for Every Context*, p. 334.
10 True Freedom Trust: http://www.truefreedomtrust.co.uk.
11 Graham Cray, *Making Disciples in Fresh Expressions of Church*, Bozeat: Fresh Expressions, 2013, p. 6.
12 Warren, *The Purpose Driven Church*, p. 102.
13 Nick Crawley: www.crossnet.org.uk/discipleship-in-community .html.
14 Encounter on the edge: http://www.churcharmy.org.uk/Groups /244969/Church_Army/Church_Army/Our_work/Research/ Encounters_on_the/Encounters_on_the.aspx.

8

Worship – when to begin and how to get started

'When are you gonna start this youth church?' asked Bob.

'We're not gonna do it, you are!' came Tracy's reply as she tried to get across the message that a Sorted worship service would not simply be set up by adults for young people but would be done with young people involved in every step of the process.

Rumblings

Throughout mid-2006, we were thinking more about setting up a youth worship service so that youngsters could experience God, hear in-depth teaching and find creative and relevant ways to worship and pray.

I was still unsure how to launch a worship service that would work and not fall flat on its face. Over recent months, I was becoming convinced that the youngsters finding faith in the small groups were going to be vital in forming the core of any congregation. It had always been our intention that a worship service would happen at some point in the journey of Sorted, but now we realized the young people would need to be involved at the heart of it, coming up with ideas and taking ownership. I felt that if they were to own it, it would be much more likely that other youngsters would come to it and discover God.

During a summer trip to Soul Survivor, two of us came away with a strong sense that God wanted us to 'wait' or 'be still' in his presence with the young people, being open to what he might want to say or do. But I knew this would be an alien concept to most of our young people, so making it work was going to need a miracle!

Following Soul Survivor, we moved out of our small cramped terrace house in Eccleshill to a semi-detached house in Idle where there was more room to breathe. Tracy now had space for a desk and Sam now had a garden to play in.

We handpicked 12 young people to meet with Tracy, Simon, Val and me in our living room so that we could plan how we were going to do a youth service. Over the summer, I had several informal conversations with some of the key young people about the idea of a worship service. They were up for it and so momentum was slowly growing. However, many of the 12 that turned up on the first night were new to the idea after having been told about it by me through a 30-second playground conversation, phone call or even just a text.

We chose Monday night because we could invite young people from the two tiny Monday-night groups and because it was a night when all four adults were available. Most young people from the two groups were keen on the worship service idea, but a couple felt it infringed on their tiny group of two people. What could we do? We only had a limited number of evenings to do youth work and forming a youth service was a God-given priority, so we sympathetically but firmly explained why this change was needed.

At our first meeting we chatted, split into two smaller groups and then came up with a plan. I suggested much of the content while giving the young people space to comment so that nothing was planned without their agreement. It wasn't a big surprise when they suggested we have a break midway through the night. This helped their concentration and proved popular for years to come. A plan evolved based on five Ws − welcome, worship, wait, wee and word. While some of these Ws are self-explanatory, 'wait' means waiting on the Holy Spirit in prayer, and 'wee' refers to the toilet break! [1]

The following week, we were ready to start our first service. I had no idea what would happen; most of the young people had never attended church services and they weren't A- (or B-) grade students used to concentrating for any length of time. Would they stick with it? Would it fall apart? I also knew if I told them off too much when they lost concentration, this would damage relationships and wreck what we were trying to build.

Our first worship service

By 7.30 p.m. next Monday, we had gathered everyone together in our living room; Tracy had just put Sam to bed as I gathered into the house the last of the smokers from just outside our front door with the plea to be quiet so that Sam could sleep.

We were still waiting for one or two latecomers. Another one or two others wanted to nip out and smoke because they had been chatting inside; it seemed we would never get everyone settled! Anyway, sure enough there we all were, cramped on our single sofa, sitting on one of the three chairs or huddled next to one another on the floor, much too close for comfort. We were finally ready to begin.

After asking everyone to be quiet, I introduced things by giving a brief explanation of what we were meeting to do and by reminding everyone what we had discussed and agreed to do the previous week. So far, so good – now it was time to put a CD song on so that we could think about the words and bring our own prayers before God in our hearts.

Almost as soon as the song started playing, the young people began chatting. I gently encouraged them to listen to the words and connect with God. After a few moments of quiet, the young people chatted again. I tried again with a bit more firmness. But after a period of quiet, guess what? The young people chatted again. They weren't being deliberately rude and I didn't want to threaten to kick anyone out because I felt we were experimenting to see what would work in helping them to connect with God in worship. This was going to be difficult!

Next, I explained a little about how God meets people with his Spirit and how we can wait on him. I then prayed aloud, inviting the Holy Spirit to come, and we all waited in silence (it felt like we were waiting for a week!). One or two young people started to whisper (I gave them a stern look that said, 'Don't even think about it'), but then after a few minutes the young people couldn't or wouldn't stay quiet any longer so conversations erupted and the waiting was over!

Looking back, the problem wasn't that the young people were badly behaved or uninterested in God, it was just that they weren't used to doing what we were doing. The nearest they ever came to it was school assembly where the threat of punishment kept them quiet. How could we make this work in a context where relationship and ownership are our biggest motivators?

Second worship service

One week later, we tried waiting on the Lord again with the young people. This time, I felt better prepared. I had been praying all week, we had quiet worship music playing in the background and we dimmed the lights. Surely prayer, quiet music and dimmed lights would create the right atmosphere to ensure that God would move by his Spirit and all would be well?

A few minutes into the night, we wait on the Spirit after I give a lengthy introduction asking the young people to focus quietly and engage with God. Little by little, voices and whispers start to happen in the darkness. My eyes and face quickly move with a piercing glance to deaden the voices with a look that says, 'You are well and truly dead if you so much as move your mouth again!' I then make the fatal mistake of closing my eyes to pray. Conversation breaks out among the group and the waiting is over again! I feel totally defeated – why isn't God doing anything? What are we doing wrong? Why won't these young people stop being normal young people and just sit silently for two minutes?

Third worship service

When the following Monday came around, there were about 17 of us gathered in my living room. One of the young people and Tracy did an interactive teaching, which worked really well. We had a break and then I started getting sweaty palms as we got ready for our 'waiting' bit! I felt it was now or never. I wasn't sure that we could keep 'waiting' with these young people if it all fell apart again.

So we all sat down and I started explaining for the third week in a row how we were going to attempt 'waiting on the Lord' (with very little faith that anything would happen). The music played quietly and we went into silence. As we started waiting, I was praying like mad, 'God, if you're going to do something, now would be a good time.' As it turned out, he seemed to agree!

As we all sat in silence, I glanced around the room. Most of the young people looked like they had finished praying; after all, we had been silent for a whole minute! Tracy looked deep in prayer, and then she suddenly looked up and whispered into to the ear of George, who was sitting next to her. I wondered what she was saying. She then started praying with the laying on of hands over George. He later described something that sounded like an experience of God (hands tingling) and then together they both prayed over his cousin Pete. The three of them then started praying for others and so, not wanting to miss the opportunity, I joined in by offering to pray with another young person. Soon everyone was getting prayed for with the laying on of hands and many of the young people sensed God's presence.

Wow! We already knew that most of our young people didn't find it easy to sit in silence and connect with God (they just weren't in the habit of doing it and hadn't grown up with it). Over the next few weeks, they started to learn to sit quietly as a group, focusing on God. We would then pray over a small number of key young people and send them to lay hands in prayer on others with the adults in support.

We basically adapted the Soul Survivor time of waiting on the Lord[2] to fit our context, so that the waiting time at the start became shorter (especially in the early days) and more emphasis was placed on releasing young people to go and pray for their peers. This worked well with youngsters who had short attention spans and were new to sitting in silence, and it fitted with the need to involve and empower young people in the process. Some people might say that we were short-changing God as he didn't get much time to guide or speak while we were waiting. However, in those early days, judging by the number of young people being blessed, he didn't seem to mind, and the times of waiting slowly length-ened as time went by.

We had outgrown our living room (it didn't take much) and moved into the church where there is more room. This method of waiting revealed to Tracy and adapted by me became the major focus of the night, and more than 50% of all the young people coming to the worship service during the first year seemed to have an experience of God. Youngsters from our small groups and beyond would come to the worship service; often seeming uninterested in the talk, they would open up to God during the prayer time as they saw their peers praying for one another – it became a time when the spiritual lights were switched on in many young lives. As the lights came on, so often their interest in God grew, as did their interest in the teaching.

Beginning worship

In those early days, our aim was simply to help the young people start the journey of becoming a worshipping commu-nity. Young people with short attention spans and almost zero church experience would need an approach to worship that was totally tailored to suit their context.

Wrestling with how Christian tradition could aid our wor-ship through its liturgy, sacraments and spiritual practices would simply have to wait for now. We did plan to connect Sorted's worship with selected parts of the Christian tradition later on (see Chapter 11).

Our aim at the beginning was much more basic: to help them encounter God, be in awe of God and keep journeying spiritually as new Christians together. Like a family in a hospital maternity ward, this wasn't the moment to decide what new clothes to buy or what GCSE options would benefit our kids. We simply had to make sure they were fed, watered and cared for! We had new spiritual babies; their survival was the only thing that mattered for now.

Keeping babies alive is relatively simple even if it's very hard work – *they simply must feed and have their most basic needs met*. Whether or not it was from the breast or baby milk products, we soon realized our spiritual babies fed on pure spiritual milk when they encountered God through prayer and the laying on of hands. This seemed to keep them engaging with worship and hungry for more.

Our 'waiting on the Lord' could make Soul Survivor seem sophisticated! We would wait briefly, begin praying for a young person or two, and then go with them to pray for others. It was often messy and chaotic, but it worked. As we prayed with them, then encouraged them to pray for each other, it was like giving out chocolate buttons in a nursery where kids enjoy the chocolate, give some away to others and cause a complete mess in the process.

On some weeks, lots of people engaged, and on others it descended into chaos. Order would come later. God didn't seem to mind the messiness, and as a loving parent he would touch, heal and meet young people constantly. As young people encountered him, they became more interested in the teaching, the Bible and prayer.

Worship and mission

One problem in many churches is that as new Christians find themselves drawn into the fabric and life of their church, they discover their relationships with non-Christians reduce over time so that their potential for evangelism becomes limited. Sadly, worship doesn't usually lead to mission!

However, the Samaritan woman discovered the true focus of worship when she met Jesus (John 4.24) and then went to tell her village, 'I have just found a man who told me everything I ever did. Do you think he might be the messiah?' (John 4.29, New Century version). Her village was soon converted. Many of our young people would encounter God, be amazed and begin to wonder whether they had discovered Jesus. We needed to create opportunities for them to share this with their peers.

Revelation 12.11 says of the apostles, 'They overcame him [the devil] by the blood of the Lamb and by the word of their testimony.' I soon discovered that if people speak openly about their new-found faith, they are less likely to hide it and often increasingly identify themselves with Jesus and his people. So I began looking for opportunities to do mini interviews with key young people about their faith, often beginning in small groups and then larger groups. Their words were brief, incomplete but genuine. Through their testimony they communicated, 'Yesterday I was just like you, then today I experienced the joy and peace of God (or saw my prayer get answered) and now I think I've found God.' Hearing this had a big effect on their mates and peers. Initially, it was sometimes hard to find one or two young people willing to speak, but after they spoke, others would also consider speaking. This was the beginning of worship causing mission.

As we formed small groups, these new Christians were willing to lead or co-lead a group. This was messy and they needed a lot of support, but they would pray, read from the Bible and explain to their peers how a prayer had been answered or why they had become a Christian. Adults sitting nearby could help explain a bit more. New young people coming to Sorted sat up and took notice. Many became open to God, some wanted us to explain the Bible to them and many would pray in the groups. Worship had led to mission!

Although messy, this is an excellent way to do mission. It also prevents a young church becoming too inward-looking. Getting new Christians to tell their testimony or lead small groups among their peers ensures that a new church doesn't just grow pastoral leaders in the new community but starts growing evangelists or pioneers at the beginning of its life, not as an 'added extra' much later on when the church suddenly realizes its need to grow.

Not all new Christians can share a testimony, but some may get involved in mission by serving or caring for new people. I wonder if the heart of Ephesians 4.11 ('It was he who gave some to be apostles, some to be prophets, some to be evangelists, and some to be pastors and teachers . . .') is about God's people serving incarnationally in a way that allows both the pioneering gifts (evangelist, apostolic) and the settler gifts (pastor, teacher) to be used together in mission, not in isolation as so often happens.

The 'serving first' model[3] makes it easier for new Christians who have journeyed initially into a 'gathering session', then on to a small group and then to encountering God in a worship service, to then go back into the 'gathering session' of a new church with their new-found faith so that they can point others to Jesus (see Figure 6).

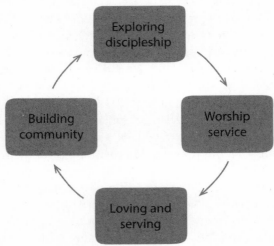

Figure 6: The 'serving first' model

People who become part of the community, grow in disciple-ship and go deeper with God in worship are often the ideal people to move from worship to mission by loving and serving in the community and/or the gathering session. These people may also be the best people to become indigenous leaders. At Sorted, these people often help out at our Friday-night session.

Worship and (trans)formation

When young people begin at Sorted, they often tell us the big social activity session on Friday evening is their favourite session. As time goes by and they come to faith, many of them say the worship session has become their favourite. Why? They are beginning to discover, like the psalmist, 'How lovely is your dwelling-place, O LORD Almighty' (Psalm 84.1).

'For where two or three come together in my name, there am I with them' (Matthew 18.20). As these young people meet together, Jesus is present and the Spirit moves among them as Jesus himself explains in this verse.

'Offer your bodies as living sacrifices, holy and pleasing to God – this is your spiritual act of worship . . . be transformed by the renewing of your mind' (Romans 12.1–2). If they learn to open themselves up to God and decide to give themselves to God in prayer as St Paul describes here, then they begin to be transformed into the likeness of Christ – a process that lasts a lifetime.

Formation is both a work of God and something we must participate in. While it should be fuelled through practising spiritual disciplines and living a lifestyle modelled on Christ, our encounters with God in worship play a big part in trans-forming us into the likeness of Jesus, as St Paul explains: 'And we, who with unveiled faces all reflect [or contemplate] the Lord's glory, are being transformed into his likeness with ever-increasing glory, which comes from the Lord, who is the Spirit' (2 Corinthians 3.18). Paul describes the worshipper looking at the Lord's glory or presence as though it were a mirror or pool of still water. As worshippers contemplate the Lord in his presence, so they are transformed and begin to reflect his glory.

As we began to worship in Sorted, the first steps were usually receiving the Spirit as someone laid on hands and prayed for the anointing of God. This reflects the truth that our faith is a free gift. As that gift expands to begin transforming the life of a new believer, so they have started a journey of formation. Contemplation, sacred space to wonder, singing, hearing the word, taking sacraments, confession, surrendering oneself to God and responding by living a life of discipleship can gradually become part of our worship and fuel our formation further.

Participation

'When you come together, everyone has a hymn, or a word of instruction, a revelation, a tongue or an interpretation' (1 Corinthians 14.26). St Paul's words suggest that everyone can participate in worship. This is harder in big congregations, but smaller fresh expressions have an opportunity to encourage their members to get involved.

Involvement could mean planning worship together, buying sound equipment together and setting up together. But it can go much further. Arts and crafts, meditation, creative worship, alternative worship, group discussion, activities and open prayer can all be used alongside the traditional ways worshippers participate, such as singing, reading the Bible, giving notices, partaking in the sacraments and being on the prayer rota.

Sorted tends to be high on participation but with intervals where one person might speak or where we all sing together. Different people of different contexts will have different preferences, but I tend to think a mix of participation with some intervals of less participation (like a short talk or solo singer) may suit people of different learning styles and cater for us introverts as well as the extraverts.

- Do the new people prefer high, medium or low levels of participation?
- What kinds of participation enable them to worship or engage with God?
- What will make a good mix of participation and less participation in your worship services?

Spontaneity

'Worship leaders go beyond ensuring that all parts of the service hold together. They create space for members of the community to hear the Spirit and share what they have heard.'[4] For years, I found it really difficult to see God at work when leading a worship service. As someone who likes a clear plan, it was hard to move away from the service plan.

Over time, I've come to realize that 'spontaneous, Spirit-led' leading is seeing what God is doing or simply creating space when God might be doing something but we're really not sure. This could mean creating space during worship for others to say a prayer, share a word or say something that might encourage or build people up. It's risky as you never know whether a person is about to say something helpful or not, but being able to rein it back in is important. If there are words, pictures or prophecies, they should be encouraged but tested out by wise and discerning Christians. (See David Pytches' *Come Holy Spirit*[5] for practical advice on how to do it.)

National leaders such as Soul Survivor founder Mike Pilavachi have done this for years at big Christian events, but we have to find our own way when operating in much smaller, local gatherings. I've slowly learnt to risk allowing others to speak, or I've gone with a gut feeling when sensing the need to pause the service plan and give space for prayer. I've found it becomes slightly easier the more I practise it.

Church services that don't allow any spontaneity could fall into the danger of holding the work of the Spirit back, whereas allowing for spontaneity can give space and focus on what the Spirit wants to do. An increasingly postmodern, interactive culture will need worship leaders to become more facilitative so that worship is both participative and spontaneous.

Have a go?

- Watch someone practise a facilitative approach to leading worship and ask how they do it.
- Practise a facilitative approach to worship where some things are pre-planned but there is space to go off script at times and allow others to share, pray and speak.
- Pray beforehand that you will discern God's promptings during a service, perhaps doing this with a couple of trusted others who have experience of hearing the Lord. Take the risk of inviting the congregation to respond to what God may be wanting. Gain experience in doing this and learn as you go.

Bite-size is good

Our culture tends to be bite-sized! Just take a look at TV adverts. Even our news stories are quick, to the point and essentially bite-sized. Working with people of no church background meant that we had to learn to do bite-size and quickly.

Most of our worship services tend to be split into small pieces otherwise minds drift. Whether it's song/notices/song/activity/break/DVD clip/short talk/prayer ministry for a service or possibly short reading/prayer/interactive activity/feedback/five-minute talk/prayer/communion or something else, we've found that breaking everything down into five- or ten-minute slots can really help people with little church experience stay focused and connected to what is happening.

Top tips for beginning worship with new people from zero church background[6]

1 *Plan it with them.* By doing it together you are achieving two purposes. First, the process of doing it together will give you an understanding of what the new people know and therefore where you need to start from. Second, planning together will involve them and let them know their views matter and will be taken into account.

2 *Pray for people to encounter God.* For us this happened through prayer and the laying on hands, but in another context it might happen through a prayerful meditation. So pray beforehand that encounters will happen and sensitively experiment with ways of engaging people with God.

3 *Choose music that helps people engage with God.* There are endless genres of Christian music. Try experimenting with different music that will enable new people to engage with God in worship. Our young people into punk and heavy metal found Christian bands playing similar music as did those into hip-hop. But we also needed music that everyone could worship to, such as popular Christian songwriter Matt Redman.

4 *Be flexible.* We began with worship music, followed by teaching, followed by prayer ministry. In the first months, we quickly brought prayer ministry nearer to the beginning so that young people would encounter God, and we found they engaged better from then on. Later on, we would introduce new things so that our worship adapted to what God was putting on our hearts and to the needs of the young people.

5 *Observe, reflect and review with the new people.* Worship was a totally new experience, so as part of the process to reassure and check the new people were still with us, we would reflect and review how worship was going. This provided both a feedback process and a space where fresh vision for worship could be shared.

6 *One step at a time.* In Chapter 11 we will explore how a young congregation can learn from the tradition and add things like sacraments, confession and liturgy gradually and context appropriately, so that it grows into maturity and depth when it's ready. Babies need milk, grown-ups need food.

7 *Depth.* As God takes the new congregation deeper, it's good to experiment by adding new things one at a time. For example, you may introduce a confession, including symbolic hand-washing coupled with teaching on forgiveness.

Connect[7]

Peter Grant tells how a fresh expression of church has developed from long-standing work among young offenders.

'The biggest surprise to us here is the worship. It was during our third session of Alpha that we decided to introduce the idea of worship at Connect. The worship leader used to be a prison governor. We were unsure how this would go down with people unfamiliar with church but simply said that "This is what Christians do". The worship leader said he'd play a song through once so everyone would get the idea of what it was like.

It was "How Great is Our God" and it was just amazing. After the first verse everyone was on their feet and going for it, it was such a God "thing" because it could never have been organized, or had such an immediate effect, if it had come from us. It was very, very, very different than any other kind of worship I have ever come across. It was raw. Our musicians are very talented but they are not polished; we have guitar, drums and sometimes piano. Our singers are young women, with incredible voices, who became Christians with us and they sing with a couple of guys.

We are now very passionate about music as a community, the worship band has come into prison to lead worship in the prison from where Connect first grew, and it's amazing to see and hear it – the guys there love singing. It sometimes sounds like a football chant. The closest description I would have is a kind of Geordie version of a black gospel church.'

Notes

1 Phil Potter's four Ws of cell church (Phil Potter, *The Challenge of Cell Church: Getting to Grips with Cell Church Values*, Oxford: BRF, 2001, p. 31) were in the back of my mind, but the idea wasn't to do the cell model, we just liked his Ws and even added some of our own!

2 See http://soulsurvivor.com/sites/default/files/soul-survivor-ministry-guidelines.pdf for more information.

3 Michael Moynagh, *Church for Every Context*, London: SCM Press, 2012, pp. 208–20.

4 Moynagh, *Church for Every Context*, p. 373.

5 See David Pytches, *Come Holy Spirit: Learning How to Minister in Power*, London: Hodder & Stoughton, 1985.

6 For creative worship ideas, see www.freshexpressions.org.uk/guide/worship.

7 Story by Peter Grant: www.freshexpressions.org.uk/stories/connect.

9

What helps people take ownership, and how can the new church learn together?

WWJD – What would Jesus do? Start a church and hand it over readymade like an IKEA flat-pack to those involved *or* form a church with the active involvement in leadership of those who attend?

The second approach may start with a model (but often won't), which is then adapted – perhaps even abandoned – by those involved. This second approach is much closer to that of Jesus. He gave them the tools to create church – his teachings, their Jewish Scriptures (our Old Testament), baptism and communion, leadership and his ongoing presence and support through the Spirit. His followers then used these tools to work out when and how they would meet, how they would remember the Last Supper, how they would do evangelism and mission and how to develop their leadership.

This second approach is riskier than the first because it means sharing the ministry with others, just like Jesus did (they baptized, Jesus didn't). However, Jesus' approach is likely to be more fruitful because what emerges is likely to be highly inculturated and empowering of the people being reached. It's also messy and means you're going to have to admit it when you need help and not be afraid to ask!

'Ownership' and 'learning together' are two topics that are tied closely together and to the second approach mentioned above. Yes, it's possible for the people of a new church to start taking ownership and get involved while learning nothing! Equally, they may learn much while being led by a 'one-man band' and have zero level of ownership.

However, when people learn together in a team context, they are more likely to get involved and develop ownership in their church. Conversely, as people start taking ownership and get involved, they are more likely to learn through the process of doing mission and church so long as they can reflect on what is happening. These two things will most likely spark each other into life, which is why this chapter puts them together.

The problem of ownership today

If I own a house then I'm more likely to spend time and money looking after it, whereas if I rent a house I might not bother because it's not my property. People begin taking responsibility, become involved and care if they have a level of ownership in a church. If we feel like our church really only belongs to the minister or larger church network, we may fall into becoming passive observers and feel disenfranchised. Just look at the political system in the UK. The belief in a 'Westminster bubble', full of corrupt politicians claiming too many expenses, aloof from the reality of daily life, led to a sense of disenfranchisement and passivity with little sense of ownership in the 2010 UK General Election.

'The church [today] has to contend with a culture of low commitment.'[1] In the western hemisphere, so much of our culture is influenced by consumerism. Younger generations have been exposed to this even more. I don't believe most people begin coming to church deliberately not wanting to get involved (although some might), but many arrive with an expectation that they are receiving a service that is being offered free of charge, as this is what our consumer culture influences us to believe. Some might mistakenly believe that money they put in the collection plate is payment for this service rather than giving from the heart. Getting involved in church and being part of the team is often counter-intuitive for many new people arriving in church.

The other cultural trait working against 'ownership' is the huge pressure on many people's time. If they are asked to get involved in an extra meeting or group, it simply sounds like another pressure on their time, rather than an opportunity to grow or become who God made them to be. This is a real pressure. Both consumerism and time pressures fight against 'ownership'.

Beth and Jade

In 2006, our Friday-night POD session moved into the local Methodist church, which has several decent-sized rooms. Unsure how to make best use of these rooms, we took young people for an initial visit to the Methodist church to find out what activities they would want to do in this space.

Chatting about the new building as they ate sweets and drank coke, Beth and Jade said the lounge room was old-fashioned and the tables were more suited to a classroom. It was a bit stuffy but still they thought the room could become a decent 'chill out' area with a good makeover.

Soon afterwards, Tracy and the girls went off to buy table cloths, table mats, fake flowers, lamps, lampshades and other bits and pieces. The girls were excited and couldn't wait to set everything up!

Next Friday, the girls arrived early with Tracy to set up the 'chill out' room. The new makeover really worked! A cafe-style atmosphere, complete with dimmed lights, nicely decorated tables and soft music, gave the room an ambiance which people wanted to be in.

Over the next few weeks, the girls enthusiastically set up the room each Friday, but then the novelty wore off and their enthusiasm waned. The adults ended up setting the room up.

Other young people had had ideas for other rooms which needed setting up and the adults found themselves doing this as well! It was becoming hard work and we were falling into the trap of 'provider–client' relationships. Something had to change.

One Friday, two adults were late getting out of work. Tracy and I couldn't set everything up on our own so Tracy told a small number of young people waiting outside for the session to open that we needed their help to set up. About six young people came in to help.

After the young people set up, they would suddenly notice when someone made a mess or carelessly damaged some equipment. 'Don't just chuck that on the floor!' said Danny to another lad. 'That belongs to our club.'

Only a couple of weeks earlier, Danny might have been one of those damaging equipment himself, but he began to care. Getting involved was causing him to take some ownership. He began to care because they began to notice!

I realized this could happen every week and so the following week I asked the young people to help again, and they did. They began to help us pack away too. As the weeks rolled on, they often reverted back into waiting for us to do it all but we persevered in asking for their help, explaining we needed their support and always thanking them for helping out, even if it was a tiny contribution. Over time, it became the natural habit of the young people to help set up and pack away, and so many began to care as ownership grew.

The strange thing is that the more they helped, the more they started to see Sorted as theirs. They began referring to the equipment and Sorted as 'ours' and would say things like, 'We should ask those new lads to be quiet.' Before this change, they would refer to Sorted as 'yours' and say to me, 'I can sell *you* these drums for *your* club.' Now they might say, 'I'll donate these drum sticks for *everyone* at *our* club.' It would need several other things to enhance the ownership but this was the starting point for many of our group.

A 16-year-old lad later summed up what we were trying to achieve: 'Some of my friends say they go to church on Sunday but what they are really saying is, they attend a church run by adults but it's different here, we don't just go to Sorted, it really is *our* church as we run it *with* you adults.'

How do I foster 'ownership'?

1 Admit you need help and don't be afraid to ask

If you're in any kind of leadership role and you want people to take ownership, you've got to be willing to share the church with them, not make all the decisions or do every important job yourself. This is hard for many of us but if we can get ourselves to that place, then we can begin to foster ownership among the people, which will lead to the growth of a much healthier church and a team that can keep the church growing even if you move on. This means I have to make myself vulnerable.

Being vulnerable means recognizing I can't do this on my own and God never intended it to be a one-man or one-woman band. One way to begin being vulnerable is to tell your people that you need their help and ask for it. Whether it's setting up equipment for a session (as in the above story) or asking others to share in the preaching, we need to admit our need for help.

Obviously, we need wisdom when we ask people for help. The Body of Christ picture is about different members having different gifts; so both recognizing gifts and timing are important, but we also need to be prepared to take some risks and give people a chance. Some adults wouldn't let young people near expensive sound equipment, but others decided to train a small number of young people, run the equipment with them and then leave them to it. They took a measured risk. Some ministers won't let members preach, but others find and encourage a member to first share a testimony, then help them lead a discussion group, before they learn how to do a short talk . . . it's a step-by-step way of learning to preach.

2 Don't take people for granted

At the end of one Sorted session, a tired adult called Fred just wanted to get the equipment away and go home to bed. 'Pick that amp up, put those footballs away!' he shouted in frustration at some young people. 'People nowadays just don't seem to realize they have a duty to help in the church,' said a vicar to me on another occasion.

I don't believe either of these approaches is helpful. New people (and some who've been around for ages) don't always notice some of the jobs that need doing. Some people don't have the confidence to do a job or they wait for someone to give them permission.

It's so much more encouraging to people if we ask politely for their help and if we genuinely thank them for what they do. This may sound like an over-obvious platitude but it's amazing how often we can forget in the heat of the moment. People respond so much better if they are genuinely appreciated and encouraged rather than if they are taken for granted.

By trying hard to ask, thank and encourage young people, we found they soon wanted to help out. This became infectious as the young people would involve others in helping out while treating them with respect and encouragement too. This all helped to enhance their sense of ownership.

3 Build a culture of ownership

For St Paul, the heart of church was mutual giving – the sharing of gifts. This only happens if there is a sense of ownership. Paul knew how to foster this ownership in the churches he planted. His letters are full of little quips: 'encourage one another', 'be kind and compassionate to one another', 'love one another', 'build one another up' and 'don't let any unwholesome talk come out of your mouths, but only what is helpful for building others up according to their needs'.

From the small beginnings mentioned in the story above, Sorted accidently developed a culture of ownership.[2] Every group begins and ends with a small team of young people setting up equipment and packing it away. This fosters ownership in every group and gives us a chance to model encouragement, kindness and compassion as we ask people to help, as we genuinely appreciate people for their contribution and as we involve people in a way that suits who they are.

It works! Young people arrive at Sorted, some who have been excluded from school, many from broken homes and others with no respect for any adults gradually start to melt as they come into a culture where people treat each other with encouragement, respect and kindness. When they trust us enough to start getting involved, they respond well to our encouragement (which is often a new experience for many) and start to feel part of the Sorted family. Belonging gradually becomes ownership as they get more involved. Equally, adults spending all week in cut-throat, dog-eat-dog work environments or who feel isolated or alone in our individualistic society will respond just as well when they enter such an environment.

Some people get involved in planning and co-leading groups. A few begin to preach and lead. This can't be done by everyone and someone should be mentored, trained and yet given permission to teach or lead. Involving indigenous people in leadership increases ownership, in that this isn't church being done *to* them or *for* them but it's church being done *with* them and *by* them.

Every Tuesday I would phone four or five older young people and ask them to help me out at the evening session. We were trying to run several small Bible groups with a lack of adults (at that time, we just had the minimum requirement for safeguarding) and so depended on several 17- to 19-year-olds for the session to function.

Richard was 18 years old and had been diagnosed with ADHD. He just didn't do discussion groups and could be disruptive to others in a group without really intending to be.

I knew I had to find a way to involve him. Sometimes, rowdy young people would turn up halfway through the groups and totally disrupt things if we let them in, so I asked him and his mate to stand by the door as stewards.

Richard did this well. Having a role in the team of protecting what we were doing gave Richard a real sense of worth. He once walked for a mile in the pouring rain to get to the session and then stand on the door for an hour!

4 Listen really well and implement people's ideas

'We should put the PA and speakers over here, set the microphone there and set up chairs . . .', explained Rob as we looked at his drawing of a room plan for the worship service.

'We'll do it exactly like that,' responded Tracy. I was a bit unsure but decided to go with it as I spotted how Rob and his mates were suddenly energized and focused on getting everything done well.

'The candles should be here, the lights can be placed in these places, the cross here and this is the order it can happen . . .', explained Courtney to the youth leader.

'Creative worship,' wrote down the youth leader on the A1 sheet.

Both these stories happened just as I've written in two different groups, several years apart. Can you spot the big difference? By listening and implementing the young person's idea, Tracy gave a whole group of young people the belief that any of them could suggest things and their ideas would be listened to, maybe even implemented. This energized and motivated them to become more involved. However, the second suggestion, spelt out in detail by Courtney, was watered down to simply 'creative worship'. Feeling disempowered and no doubt thinking it pointless to suggest anything else, Courtney slumped back in her seat!

I find it a real effort to listen well and implement someone's idea. I usually think of ten reasons why it should be done differently from what they've suggested! Sometimes it's better to go with someone's idea even if you're only half convinced. Not only does it tell them you really are open to their ideas but it gives people a chance to try something and either be successful or learn through failure. Church can only truly be owned if people are given the chance to suggest and act upon some of their own ideas.

'We want to join the two groups together,' said Ronnie. I explained why two teenagers leading the twenty young people as a small group wouldn't work, but both Ronnie and the other three young leaders were desperate to try and were convinced they could do it. So I let them! The following week, they joined up the two groups and simply couldn't keep control, let alone hold a discussion about God. I didn't say a word. They had learnt through the experience why a small group needs to be small to function. Even though they were discouraged, I reckon it was better to let them try something. The sheer number of adults who sit passively in church tells me that we need to do much more to create a climate of permission-giving, and, 'It's OK to fail because we learn through failure.'

5 Suggest ideas and let others take the credit

Years ago a mentor said, tongue in cheek, 'Sometimes you have to suggest a little idea to young people, let them play around with it and then run with it until they think it's their idea.' This wasn't meant as an insult to young people but something about the art of empowering, enabling leadership.

A leader's job isn't to come up with every idea to solve every problem. This is difficult for some of us, especially if we're 'ideas' or 'plant' people (see, for example, the Belbin team roles in[2]). If this describes you, perhaps try sharing a couple of ideas briefly, but don't share them fully formed, planned to the nth degree. Give others the chance to reject or contribute to an idea so that it might become a team's idea not just an individual's idea. Once the team wants to implement an idea, you can always plan it out to the nth degree together.

Sometimes leaders do need ideas up their sleeves or to plan an idea to the nth degree, explaining to others why something is necessary. But it's not good to do this all the time. Leaders must choose what to 'own' and what others should 'own'. I chose the teaching at our discussion group but deliberately let young people choose what we did during the social time so that choices were shared. A minister may prayerfully choose which subject to preach on but he or she doesn't need to decide what theme to base the parish social around or which venue to choose for the parish weekend away.

Others must be encouraged to share their ideas too. Sometimes indigenous people have great ideas because they understand the local context better than an outside leader. Young people often shared insights that shaped or moulded our ideas in Sorted because they instinctively knew how other young people would respond better than we did.

6 Body of Christ functioning well

The Church belongs to Jesus, and the New Testament pictures different members of the Body of Christ working together, led by Jesus. Jesus entrusts us with his Church of which we are stewards. This is teamwork with Jesus as team leader. Yes, human leadership is important but team members must be enfranchised, involved and listened to.

When Christians pray together, allow the Spirit to guide them and then serve Jesus by using the spiritual gifts listed in 1 Corinthians 12, the gifts of service listed in Romans 12 or the gifts for building the church listed in Ephesians 4; then this in itself can foster the deepest sense of ownership. The group prays and discerns together and each person uses their God-given gift with a clear sense that they are serving Jesus. We should aim to take people to the place of listening prayer and Spirit-empowered service. We've discovered this is messy among new people as some will be able to join in and discover God using them while others will take much longer, and so this is a gradual process of people slowly learning to connect to God and discover his gifting.

The leader's role includes discerning what the Spirit is saying and how the various gifts work in a complementary way towards fulfilling the church's vision. It's important the leader doesn't allow people to become unaccountable to Scripture or each other yet he or she must not stifle the gifts by putting a straightjacket on the team in terms of what they can or can't do.

7 *Organic to organization*

In a smaller group, it's often easier to foster ownership because it's easier to hold discussions, give everyone a chance to contribute and get involved. This can be harder in larger groups and explains why there has been a realization of the importance of small groups to enable deeper community life, whether it's through cell church model,[4] Willow Creek model[5] or the use of small groups in courses such as Alpha or Start. This raises the question – how do we continue to foster ownership to new people as a group or congregation grows larger?

Encouraging small groups is important, but there are other things we can do too. Our early sessions were attended by small numbers and so asking people to help set up equipment and so on could be done on an ad hoc basis on the night and gave time to experiment and learn about ownership.

As the groups grew, we suddenly found that peer pressure could prevent young people from helping out and so they would stand and watch us set up just like a large congregation of adults will watch a small number of folk preparing for the service. Large numbers seem to make it harder for people to join in unless specifically invited.

Our solution was to gather a small team of young people to meet to set up and have a team meeting for the session before everyone arrived; these young leaders were to encourage others to help too. Some did, but some tried to stop others helping just like the disciples once tried to stop people helping Jesus. I usually had to pick up the young team by car so they would be there on time.

The other solution to stop large numbers preventing ownership is to simply reproduce a group when you reach a certain size. Ownership and community life by their very nature are hard to foster in large groups, and so reproducing elsewhere or halving a group in order to reproduce and keep growing might be a solution.

Connect[5]

Peter Grant, working with a young offender fresh expression, sums up ownership:

> A sense of ownership is something that has always been part of all that happens here. Right from the very start of Alpha, people went into the kitchens and started helping and then tidying up afterwards, they didn't have to be asked. That kind of 'come and be involved' approach is part of who we are and what we do; it's all about doing things *together* and not *for*. Connect is not something that's 'put on' by the church, instead that sense of ownership prompts many people to share their testimony and has encouraged people to discover – and use – their gifts.

Learning together

One barrier to learning occurs when people look at something fruitful such as Alpha or Messy Church and think 'let's just do that' without really asking why it's fruitful and how it might work in their context. Without understanding how it works or without adapting it to context, there is a good chance it could flop or become unfruitful. It's important we try to understand why things work and why they don't, praying for wisdom and understanding, learning together as we go.

Another barrier to learning occurs when people stick with what they're doing because 'We've always done it that way'. This is really saying, 'We don't want to think and change because that's uncomfortable, hard work or simply too risky.'

If we don't find ways to think, reflect and learn together, there's a good chance we'll keep making the same mistakes and find ourselves going round in circles!

Just think what might happen if the reverse were true: if a group of people learn what works and why as they do mission and form church, then some will be able to lead having learnt and understood the vision and values. Others will be able to start new groups with the DNA they've learnt and experienced. When problems arise, there will be more people equipped with the learning needed that will help everyone to problem-solve. In other words, it's a no brainer! It's vital we learn together as we do mission and church – but how?

Trapped in the maze!

'How's your night been?' asked my next door neighbour as I got out of the car after a tough Sorted session.

'Could have been better; I can't make sense of young people! Sorted is just hard work!' I replied.

'Do you want a beer?' he asked as he stood on his doorstep supping a can. He could see I was stressed. I accepted his offer.

To be truthful, the evening hadn't been that bad. My problem was that I didn't really understand what was going on – why did young people engage one week, then misbehave the next? Why did some help out one week, but not the next? How did we solve the issue of negative peer pressure? How did we get them interested in God? How will we ever form a real community with God in the mix among this lot? I had no answers to these questions and it was really making me doubt that we could form a youth church.

I'd read books on mission and fresh expressions, we'd got a flexible vision and simple values, which were right for these young people, but connecting this to the actual youth work was difficult. I was beginning to understand the young people and their culture but couldn't work out how to make youth church work among them. Ownership would be a huge part of the answer but there were many other things too.

I'd been writing session reports after each session to record numbers, incidents and issues, both for safeguarding purposes and so we would know of young people who needed contacting later on. As I wrote the session reports, I began to play around a bit.

As I prayed, I would jot down anything that had a positive or negative effect, however small or insignificant it might seem. I began to question what caused it to happen. For example, if the young people really engaged, was it because of how we presented it? Was it because we were more interactive? Was it due to someone being missing who might disrupt? The more I asked questions, the more I started to see little patterns emerge. This was the beginning of starting to understand what was going on in front of me.

As these patterns emerged, I began to experiment. For example, if I rang an influential young person and asked them to help me with a small job, I could then observe what effect this had on his or her peers afterwards.

Different numbers of young people at a session would totally change the group dynamics and so we began experimenting with slightly different approaches for different-sized groups. We learnt that groups of 20 to 40 young people function better with a little team of young helpers (4 or 5 helpers in a group of 20, 8 to 10 helpers in a group of 40) and by finding ways to involve the most influential young people by giving each of them a role. They would do notices, lead small groups, help run the tuck shop, set up equipment and meet outside the big group to plan sessions. These little changes had a huge impact on how a session functioned.

Learning happened through the many conversations going on, especially between Tracy, Val, Simon and me as we met over a meal. Val would get words from God and Simon brought his experience of business management into the conversation. Stuart Hacking, the school chaplain, was gifted at understanding how young individuals ticked and how to pastorally care for them, while Tony Brown brought his experience of working with teens both as a teacher and as a youth worker. In our management group meetings, Steve Hollinghurst had wide experience of fresh expressions and David Lee had years of mission experience. They would ask the hard questions that required us to re-examine what we were doing and tweak our approach.

I would try to discern what God might be saying through other people, discard what didn't fit the youth work experience we were gaining, and figure out how to action new insights. Occasionally we would adapt plans immediately but often it was about introducing something slowly. I found journalling helped me enormously with this process. Getting thoughts on to paper, asking questions of them and forming little plans helped me to make sense of what I heard from others and begin to plan a way ahead.

New insights and learning were fed back to the volunteer team who would help us test things out. It was important to listen to them as much as possible to gain understanding, and so team members felt encouraged to share and become excited by what they were learning.

Team meetings included space to pray and listen to God. It was important not to rely on our own wisdom but to humbly give space for God to guide. We were careful to test and weigh guidance but we always took it seriously. Val had a word from God that he was going to teach us as we did Sorted. The message was to take one step at a time and enjoy learning through each stage of the journey. As this happens, the learning is both retained and yet continues to be refined. We pass it on to others and, as they put it into practice, they often have a new angle on it with fresh insights.

Can we guarantee learning will happen?

In a word – no! But we can put things in place to greatly increase the chances of us learning together. Here are some pointers to make it happen.

Team meetings

'One of the greatest myths of entrepreneurship has been the notion of the entrepreneur as a lone hero . . . the reality is that successful entrepreneurs either built teams about them or were part of a team throughout.'[7] If teams are a massive part of doing mission and church well, then team meetings have to be set up in such a way that encourages learning to happen.

Team training at the start of a pioneering venture can provide a set of foundation stones to build the new church on. As the church is built, we can learn by comparing our experience to the initial training. So we might all learn about discipleship during training and then, as the church is built, people begin to spot where discipleship is happening or ask why they can't see it. Training expands horizons, inspires vision and increases the expectation of God doing a new thing, but it also helps the team to look out for the things they've done in training.

The relationships within a team will influence its ability to learn. Love, honesty, mutual respect, humour and a light atmosphere can give people confidence to say what they think, knowing they will be listened to and not shot down in flames. If we create this environment by modelling it, it's highly likely we will help others to learn. Leaders should model good listening so that the tone of team meetings includes listening respectfully and isn't full of interruptions.

We found that teams learn together when there is a framework for learning:

- prayer
- vision reminders
- feedback from the team on how they feel different activities are going
- solution-finding to problems
- planning time together.

We might spend 10–15 minutes only on each of the above but doing this regularly within a 'framework for learning' enables teams to reflect on what is happening, learn from it and figure out the next step.

When Tracy took the Sorted DNA into a parish church, she immediately changed the PCC agenda. Until this point, conversations about mission were an added extra at best. The new agenda started with prayer and then 45 minutes discussing mission, including sharing of recent good news stories, identifying current problems, time to problem-solve and make brief plans going forward. Nuts and bolts issues were then discussed after the coffee break. This meant that mission was not only given time but discussed as first priority at the beginning when everyone was still awake!

Leaders can help learning to happen by keeping the vision and values clear, simple and yet flexible. If this is missing, conversations about mission and learning can become a free-for-all, a bit like students veering into discussing French during a Maths lesson.

Prayer and Scripture

God is our ultimate teacher; it's important that we seek to learn from him. We may apply some of the tools of secular education to our work, such as action-reflection learning or gaining insights from the disciplines of sociology or psychology, but 'Unless the LORD builds the house, its builders labour in vain' (Psalm 127.1). God can teach us a lot through secular education, disciplines of the 'ologies', and much more besides, but our learning will bear fruit if it is rooted in listening prayer.

Some of our teams are blessed with people who receive words and pictures from God. With good discernment, it becomes possible for words and pictures given over time to form a narrative that we can measure against the work on the ground. This can strengthen our faith that God is in control and be a tremendous source of encouragement and learning for a team to be able to see how God is taking them on a journey. It keeps us humble, open and seeking after God. It gives us confidence that God is doing something.

Any record of words and pictures needs to be rooted in reality, not disconnected from what is happening on the ground, otherwise some in the team will find this 'spiritualism' a distraction from the job in hand. The first letter to the Thessalonians 5.20

tells us, 'do not treat prophecies with contempt. Test everything.' While gaining much encouragement myself from words and pictures, I've not always managed to enable a whole team to gain encouragement and sometimes wish I had spent time jotting down the words/pictures and then helping others in the team to make sense of the guidance by connecting it to the pioneering work.

Other teams don't have members regularly receiving words/ pictures from God but they do intercede faithfully for people and situations. As their intercessory prayer bears fruit, it's important these team members hear about the answers to their prayers so they can be encouraged by knowing God is at work.

Mike Moynagh observes how the early Christians reflected on the Hebrew Scriptures to provide practical pastoral guidance to their hearers: 'Reflection on experience was the seedbed of doctrine . . . [We] will learn essential doctrines most effectively as part of truthful reflection on life's experiences and how Jesus connects to them.'[8]

Reflecting on experience and drawing parallels to Scripture can help us gain a Godly perspective on our work, challenge us to live up to what we read and yet encourage us with the knowledge we are in line with the Bible. As we see what God is doing, this can give us a new paradigm with which to view familiar passages and they in turn can give us fresh insights.

Reflection, discussion and planning

As the rain poured and the darkness fell, so the young people drifted off home. We were worried! This was the third week in a row this had happened at our Friday-night session at the POD. What had worked so well on dry summer nights with plenty of sunlight was fast becoming unworkable by early October.

With up to 30 young people at the session, we needed use of the outdoor grounds of the school for games, skateboarding or chilling. Thirty people in the POD was way too cramped for more than a few minutes at a time, but wet weather was making outdoor activities unworkable and the young people left!

Disappointment was palpable. Two volunteers thought this could be curtains for Sorted.

It had taken so long just to gather a group of this size and now we were losing it. After the session, the conversation among the team was brief – we simply had to find a suitable building for the group, and fast! There was no point discussing it much beyond this fact until we had some places to view.

On Monday morning I began several days of phoning and visiting any and every possible venue that might be suitable. Twelve buildings later, with eleven unsuitable or unavailable, there was the Methodist church just round the corner. A popular community facility, I couldn't imagine it would be available but I had to give it a try.

They had one free slot during the whole week, which just happened to be a Friday night! As I contacted the booking secretary, a visit was hastily arranged. Despite being impressed by the four large rooms, I had plenty of questions. Will young people come into a church? Will they wreck it? Can we 'police' a building of this size? There was nothing to wreck in the POD and little to keep an eye on.

Tracy and I visited the church and noted all the pros and cons while expressing our interest in Sorted wanting to use the building. A meeting was set up with the church elders.

In the meantime, we fed back our findings to the volunteer team. There were big positives but also many questions about whether we could use this facility for 30 young people, many with challenging behaviour. The size was good and it was only a five-minute walk from the POD, making it easy to direct our group to. Of all 12 venues, it was in the best location, being close to the school and easy for young people to find. As its one available weekly slot was a Friday night, this made us think God was at work. We had to give it a go!

We had to wait two long months before we could use the Methodist church. This meant sitting it out in the POD and making the best of a bad situation. We had to adapt our vision to suit where we were at – with a reduced group of about ten young people making use of the POD.

We had to think on our feet. Outdoor sports were out due to the weather, and so we improvised: I dragged in a screen and video projector for a film night, Simon brought a stove and cooked hot dogs, game consoles were shipped in and out for a night, as we tried to adapt the session to the new situation. Reflection, discussion and planning happened after the session, over the phone and mostly on the hoof as we just about hung on to the remainder of our group.

In the New Year, we began in the Methodist church. Once again, we had to adapt quickly and think on our feet. The big building threw up the immediate problem of too many rooms to oversee and plenty of stuff to misuse or abuse. Keys were quickly requested from the church and locks installed so that unused rooms could be locked off from access. The wheelchair had to be hidden in a broom cupboard otherwise it might be damaged because everyone wanted a free ride!

As numbers quickly grew, preventing damage to the building or equipment was the next problem. A fire extinguisher was set off, costing Sorted money and the trust of the church. Quick thinking and emergency team meetings led us to react with a message of 'choose it or lose it' to the group of young people as we figured out how to toughen up on bad behaviour while not destroying relationships in the process. Two-week bans were introduced. As the first young person was banned, I followed up by checking if he was OK and reminding him that he is important and we still wanted him to be part of Sorted when he returned. We learnt that it's good to ban (it curbs wrongdoing) and it's even better to follow up with care (the young person feels able to return and usually starts respecting us).[9]

Before the POD session started in April 2005, I spent too much time thinking how to connect our vision to the young people, perhaps making it over-complicated. It was only when I threw myself into the schools work, and then the POD session took off, that I had enough experience coming my way to begin to reflect, discuss and plan with the team (often on the hoof!).

The landscape under our feet changed three times in the space of a year and this threw up totally different challenges. Here is a quick timeline:

- **April 2005.** We begin gathering young people as Tony and I invite them to the POD session = young people start arriving each week.
- **July 2005.** Thirty young people are now attending the POD session but some young people continually disrupt our 'God talks'. Reflection – Discussion – Planning (R – D – P) teaches us to be more interactive and to involve young people themselves in the talk slots = listening and respect begins improving.
- **October 2005.** Dark and wet nights cause young people to leave. R – D – P leads us to start finding a new venue. After gaining use of the Methodist church, we find we can't use it until January = we do have a venue on the horizon.
- **November–December 2005.** We now have ten young people and can't do outdoor activities. R – D – P causes us to improvise, bringing various bits of equipment each week to the POD for indoor activities = we keep together the group of ten, others join us and so all is not lost to the wet nights.
- **January 2006.** We begin in the Methodist church but too many rooms means that young people run riot. R – D – P causes us to ask church elders for locks and keys = issue of too many rooms solved.
- **February 2006.** We are struggling to protect equipment and the building as a fire extinguisher is set off deliberately by a young person. R – D – P leads to 'choose it or lose it' policy of two-week bans plus pastoral care follow-up = respect increases and young people help put ground rules in place, bad behaviour subsides among regular young people.
- **April 2006.** Beth and Jade 'make over' a room but we adults soon find ourselves setting up all the equipment and falling into 'provider–client' relationships. R – D – P causes us to start asking young people to help set up and pack away. Later this will become young teams = young people begin taking more ownership within Sorted.

We learnt much more during this year than we had learnt during the previous 12 months. Going through these experiences meant we had to think on our feet, say our prayers and practise R – D – P all the time!

Learning has power to change situations

When all this was happening, we might easily have lost our way or given up. The team training provided the foundation and so we kept coming back to it. While the general principles remained true, much of the practical outworking had to be relearnt. For example, ownership was a principle we always wanted to put into practice but it was only after living through the stories in this chapter that we knew how to encourage ownership to take place. From then on, all our groups have benefited hugely from the learning that we gleaned after living through these stories.

Patricia Shaw suggests:

> Rather than making sense of our experience, sense making is part of the movement in our experience. Individuals can't stand outside the whole and describe it as a given because the very description changes what is described. The general and his commanders aren't surveying a landscape outside the battlefield, it is under their feet, changing as they walk and interact with it. The territory of exploration is formed by the exploration itself.[9]

As we travelled together through that eventful year, our learning together shaped the future landscapes we were to walk upon. For example, involving young people in setting up and packing away happens from day one in all Sorted groups and a culture of ownership begins to form sooner.

Missio Dei[11] tells us that mission happens as we respond to what God is doing and join in. The story above shows how we had to travel the learning loop many times as we reflected and discussed our experience before planning our next move. On the one hand, we were reacting to changes in the landscape and planning our next move. Yet we were also shaping the landscape to come as we joined the God already working on the landscape. And so every added prayer, every conversation with a young person, every relationship built, every positive perspective we learnt and shared with the team, every act of kindness and love that would all shape the landscape to come.

The Stowe[12]

Baptist pioneer minister Ali Boulton describes how her team learnt together both by listening to God and through their experiences. Here is an excerpt from her article describing this learning journey.

'I felt that God had said some specific things to us:

- first, I felt that God had said not to talk about him. It seemed like a strange missional strategy but more people came and talked to me about faith than ever before in my Christian life, which was amazing! Later, when we had some opposition to the Christian presence in the area, people commented that I had never imposed my faith on anyone. This was important as, by then, people had become Christians and a church for the unchurched had emerged.
- secondly, I felt that God had said that he would tell us what to do through the community. This became very significant as time went on. I guess we just set about making friends with people. Some people wanted to exchange numbers, meet for coffee and set up a Facebook group. We organized a community fun day alongside the housing association and in response to our neighbours, organized community games.

After the community day, more people got in touch. Within a few days I was contacted for the first time by someone on the brink of suicide – this has become a key part of my ministry on the estate.

I also had some women come to my door saying, 'We loved the community day; will you organize a Halloween party next?' We struggled with that as none of us believed in celebrating Halloween but God had told us to unconditionally bless the community − all faiths and none − he had also told us that he would tell us what to do through the community. After much prayer, and the verse from Acts 10 telling Peter not to call things unclean which God has made clean, we did the party. One of my teenagers commented, 'Mum thinks she has claimed back pumpkins for God; he thought he had them already.'

It was at the Halloween party that someone said, 'Do you know what I'd like? Wouldn't it be lovely if you did us a nativity play with all the children?' This ended up as a big outdoor community event. If we had said no to Halloween, I think that would have shut the door. The Halloween party is now an annual event.

We continued to serve the community in response to, and alongside, the people around us. Mostly starting in our house, we set up a toddler group, coffee morning, a toddler lunch club, a youth club, after school club and amazingly we were asked to start a God club for the kids on a Sunday afternoon. There isn't space to share that whole story!

Our first Easter there, in 2010, was amazing. Some people were chatting about Easter and in response to some comment I made, I was asked if Easter was a 'God thing?' To cut a long story short, we put on some activities on Good Friday morning to explore the Christian story of Easter in the portacabin. We expected a few kids or families but about 50 people with no church background came along. It was a very special time. As a result I invited people to join us on Easter Sunday morning and 35 people joined us.

We thought we would do it again at Pentecost – but God reminded us that he was in control and would tell us what to do through the community. So ten days after Easter, someone said she had enjoyed church on Easter day at our house so much, could she come every week? Of course we didn't have a church but as I tried to think what to say she filled in the blanks! '10.30, your house on Sunday?' 'Sure!' And so the next Sunday, church began. The lady who asked me has never been, but that first Sunday, two families came and we saw our first person become a Christian a couple of weeks later on 24th April. We saw her life transform and she was the first to be baptized. Praise God we have seen others come to faith and be baptized too.'

Finally, ownership and learning will increase as we practise listening prayer, train as a team and share ideas when we meet together. Yet we learn mostly by stepping out and giving things a try. Our experiences should cause us to travel the learning loop of reflection, discussion and planning our next move. But we must not forget that our words and actions are continually shaping the context we find ourselves part of. Perhaps another crucial lesson is learnt as we let the indigenous people get involved so they can begin to learn and to teach us what mission and church look like in their culture.

Notes

1 Michael Moynagh, *Church for Every Context*, London: SCM Press, 2012, p. 341.
2 We always intended to foster as much ownership as possible but the way it came about war accidental in that we didn't plan it that way.
3 Moynagh, *Church for Every Context*, p. 307.

4 Cell church is a church made up of cells or small groups. Many use the format of four 'W's (welcome, worship, word and witness) to structure their meetings. For more information, go to www.acpi.org.uk/acuk for the website of the Anglican cell church network.

5 Willow Creek is a North American church started by Bell Hybels that puts a huge emphasis on the importance of doing community in small groups. For more information, go to www.willowcreek.org.

6 Peter Grant, https://www.freshexpressions.org.uk/stories/connect.

7 T. Cooney in Moynagh, *Church for Every Context*, p. 29.

8 Moynagh, *Church for Every Context*, p. 242.

9 Moynagh argues that planning as learning is better than planning as analysis (*Church for Every Context*, p. 284). Drawing on the findings of complexity theorists, he argues that the world is often chaotic, with the landscape continually changing under our feet. As we try out new ideas, often we reflect/discuss and then plan as we go. Henry Mintzberg (in Moynagh, *Church for Every Context*) suggests we learn as we act, and so good strategies are formed as people try things out.

10 Patricia Shaw in Moynagh, *Church for Every Context*, p. 301.

11 Graham Cray (ed.), *Mission-Shaped Church* (London: Church House Publishing, 2004, p. 85) explains *Missio Dei*.

12 Story by Ali Boulton: https://www.freshexpressions.org.uk/stories/stowe.

PART 4

Looking further ahead

10

How do we reproduce a fresh expression of church?

One big obstacle to reproducing a church is the inability to 'see' when God wants us to reproduce. Another big obstacle is dismissing an idea to reproduce out of hand immediately because the challenges of where to find the people, time, money, buildings and leadership needed can appear insurmountable. Even if a pioneer can 'see', getting others to 'see' can be another large obstacle.

Starting again

'Do you fancy helping me with some schools work in Hanson?' asked Tony during a busy session in late 2006.

'Sorry, I'm far too busy with Sorted 1 at the moment!' was my unenthusiastic response.

Sorted 1 had only recently added the 'worship' stage and a leader had just advised me to consolidate our work, not add to it. What's more, I just couldn't see where the resources would come from to begin new schools work, let alone reproduce Sorted elsewhere.

In March 2007, someone suggested I start doing youth work in Hanson Academy, which is a mile up the road from Immanuel College and Sorted 1. My initial reaction was, 'I'm too busy running Sorted 1 and doing youth work in Immanuel to get involved in Hanson.' However, thoughts of the invitation to get involved in Hanson wouldn't go away; it stayed in my mind, so that in the weeks following the meeting, I asked a couple of prayerful women from a local church to pray about 'Hanson' in case God might speak to one of them.

An opening door . . .

'Andy, I was praying and saw in a vision you were being given a key to unlock a door to a mission field that has been closed for a long time and the message is that God is going to open the door to this mission field and no one is going to be able to close it,' came the response a week later from one of the women.

A request then came to Tony for someone from outside the school to take over the small Christian Union because its one leader (a PE teacher) was leaving Hanson in a month's time. This provided a window of opportunity. I immediately began helping out at the Christian Union in Hanson with a view to co-leading it (with Tony Brown) when the CU leader moved on during the summer break. It then took an encouraging phone call from the head teacher of Immanuel to convince the head teacher of Hanson that Tony and I were safe enough to take over the CU. The door was opening and our prayers seemed to be getting answered concerning Hanson!

I began to wonder if God wanted us to start a second youth church. But I had lots of questions, such as 'Will the local churches around Hanson support us?' Yet my biggest question was, 'How can we manage to run two youth churches with our existing team when running one was hard enough?'

Hanson is a large state school with no chaplain (unlike Immanuel) to help us get established in the school. It has very little Christian presence and its leadership at the time were wary of specific faith groups coming into school because they didn't want to upset parents of other faith groups represented in the school. It would need careful handling. Hanson is busier than Immanuel so visitors are less noticeable in its mass of people. There was no church school ethos and we had no natural supporters among the staff, as they all seemed too busy to spend time supporting anyone. So we had to work with whichever contacts came our way and pray for God to keep opening doors of opportunity in school. Getting hold of any senior staff was hard work.

Another open door

We were allowed to run a Christian Union once a week in one specific room but we weren't allowed to contact young people in the playground about our club (in case someone were to accuse us of pushing Christianity at young people) while doing detached youth work. During the first few weeks, we just hoped young people from the previous year's Christian Union would be the starting point for our new lunch club. However, only one young person, John, came to the club.

As the first half-term progressed, despite a Year 7 assembly and some posters designed by John, he continued to be the only young person attending our lunch club. With very few opportunities to engage with the young people in the school and only a once-a-week Christian Union in an 'off the beaten track' corner of the school, our chances were not looking good! This caused a fair bit of desperation before God.

One day, I was in my office on my knees reminding God that he was opening this door into Hanson. I asked him to show us how to get the young people to come to our lunch club. As I was praying, I sensed the Holy Spirit nudging me with the thought that I should pray with John and then send him out of the lunch club to invite his friends to come to the club. It was as though God was saying, 'Andy, in Immanuel, to find people of peace, you would walk round the playground – in Hanson, send John to find the people of peace.'

Two days later, I arrived at Hanson for our weekly lunch club and John arrived on his own again. After I explained the idea to him, he seemed to like it and so I prayed for him and he went out to find some friends. A few minutes later, John brought back three mates and we all played football with a softball. From then on, each week new people arrived!

Over the next three months, the number of young people attending the lunch club grew to over 20. It seemed that the younger guys within the group (which included John's friends) were those we were starting to build relationships with. After more conversations with them, we formed a second lunch club around watching films for the younger boys, with the aim of deepening relationships.

A Sorted 2?

Approaching the local churches would be make or break. If they didn't like the idea of Sorted starting in their area, or if they believed in traditional church youth work only, then the whole idea would be a non-starter. The truth is that we needed their support to make a youth church happen. This was a big deal and so I asked several trusted people to pray. A second youth church had to be a collaborative effort; the local churches had to support it through contributing prayers, people, premises and pounds. The church leaders needed to be up for it!

In January 2008, I went to visit the leader of the biggest Anglican church in the Hanson area. Paul Walker is a man with a big heart who says what he thinks. I figured that if he were to support the vision, other church leaders might support it too.

I shared with Paul what had happened in the previous few months at Hanson and the vision of a second youth church. Paul told me how impossible it had been for any Christians to get into Hanson over ten years (confirming the woman's vision – unknown to him at the time) and how the churches simply weren't reaching young people in the area or in Hanson. He felt the churches needed a new opportunity to reach the local young people. Having heard about Sorted 1, he was keen for us to start something similar. He suggested we call it Sorted 2 so that people knew what it represented. So from that moment on, it became Sorted 2!

A week later, Paul and I were sitting in his lounge, sipping tea and chatting to several other church leaders of various denominations and church networks about Sorted 2. Things went extremely well. All the leaders were supportive and enthusiastic. Maybe it was because the four churches had already experienced working together in mission. Maybe it was because Hanson was like a small city (slap bang in the middle of two of the parishes) whose walls had previously been impossible to climb, but now here was a real chance to reach out in mission to lots of young people using a model that had already been fruitful. Whatever the reason, things were looking really positive and all four churches pledged financial support, offered to pray and let us use their premises. All four leaders pledged to chat to people in their congregations who might be potential volunteers in a Sorted 2 adult team. These people were so supportive and I was so glad!

Several months passed as the church leaders shared the vision with their churches. I preached and gave a notice at two of the churches. We soon recruited a team of about ten people. Some of these volunteers were people who had run the church youth group in the past, others responded to an invitation from the pulpit to help, and still others were handpicked by their church leaders. I only knew one of these volunteers – what would they be like? Would they be open to the vision and values of Sorted?

The church leaders whom they sent my way were pretty wise, but this method of finding volunteers wasn't foolproof! Some would be suitable, some would become suitable through teaching, some wouldn't be suitable but would be OK as helpers to make up the numbers, and some just couldn't be part of the team. As it turned out, the church leaders had recruited 'safe' people to work with young people, but by allowing others to choose the volunteers, it was harder to make sure they got the vision and values. Training became even more important.

With one youth church already running and Tracy just starting her curacy, spare evenings to meet the volunteer team were extremely limited. The only free night was a Friday night. I had recently pulled out of the Friday-night session of Sorted 1 (See Chapter 12 for the story of how, as the pioneer, I gradually left Sorted 1 to start Sorted 2, and how Tracy as a settler gradually took over Sorted 1) and we knew Friday would be a good night for young people when we were ready to run a session for Sorted 2.

Fortunately, all the volunteers could make Fridays, although most of them were extremely busy, so we started meeting every other week.

Second time round

It was easier doing things second time around. I looked at the training material I had used the first time round, modified it, scrapped quite a lot of it and added some things. Most importantly, I now had lots of real-life stories of situations from the past five years to add to the theory. The vision and values were easier to understand because there was a living example of the vision and values being practised a mile away.

The flipside of the coin was the risk we would fall into the trap of mimicking Sorted 1 too much and not make decisions about the development of Sorted 2 based on its mission context. For me personally, the danger when I was asked questions about our plans, or about a specific issue, would be to say too often, 'In Sorted 1 we did it this way . . .', rather than asking questions about the young people from Hanson and consulting with them.

There were differences between the Sorted 1 and Sorted 2 volunteer teams. The Sorted 1 team were mostly on the fringe of local churches, whereas the Sorted 2 team was full of PCC members, heavily involved in local church life. For PCC members used to discussions, decisions and a plan for the way ahead, they had to learn that plans needed to be flexible as we listened to young people and adapted to their needs. For others, it was learning to change their expectations of 'how young people are supposed to behave'.

We had to learn afresh to put young people first – it had to be about their needs, their aspirations and developing Sorted 2 with them. It took a while for one or two volunteers to get the idea that Sorted is 'by young people, for young people' not 'by adults, for young people'.

As before, many months were spent meeting to worship, pray, train and get to know each other as a vital prelude for building trust and coming towards a shared vision and values.

Sorted 3 – reproducing differently

'Why are no new young people coming any more?' asked Abigail one Friday night.

Discontent grew in the Sorted camp as Sorted 1 got older and new young people stopped coming to the sessions from Immanuel College. By 2012, Sorted 1's youngest member was now 17. A report came through of some young teens turning up at our Friday session and then turning away at the sight of several 18- or 19-year-olds hanging outside the main door smoking. The message being portrayed was that this was a group for young adults not younger teens. It could not have been clearer had the message been written down and stuck on the door itself!

We were now unsuitable to cater for school-age teens and this was a big headache. The flipside of the coin didn't look much better either – the number of 17–20-year-olds was decreasing each Friday. It didn't take an Einstein to work out why! Most young adults will socialize in a pub or club each Friday night, and so it was the wrong night of the week to bring new young adults into Sorted 1 and grow the group. Many Sorted 1 young adults had already opted for the pub on Fridays anyway. We were losing both the younger teens and the younger adults, all at the same time by being in this situation; something had to change.

We began having conversations over several months with both young adults and adult volunteers of Sorted 1. The adult volunteers needed a sense of hope that we would work with younger teens again. Two of the volunteers had sons whom they hoped might get involved in any new younger teen group. However, the Sorted 1 young adults didn't want to lose their group and sense of family.

Damien Hine had joined us that summer from Church Army. Damien's gifts were in pioneering, so we came up with a plan to move the Sorted 1 Friday-night session into a different venue on a Sunday night with the hope it would provide a space for new young adults to join our existing group. It would be wrong to say this was an easy move – some of the young adults had spent six years being part of Sorted 1 and they felt that a key part of its identity was tied up in the Friday-night session. Most were open to change but we spent a lot of time trying to reassure a few and give them hope that this was a new chapter and not the end of the story for them. We hadn't taken the decision lightly and had sought to involve, consult and listen throughout the process, but it had to happen.

This left us with the Friday-night venue free for us to begin a Sorted 3 by getting alongside younger teens in the school, which was just round the corner. Quite a few of the adult volunteers formed part of a new team, as did some young adults who wanted to 'give something back' after all that had been done for them via Sorted 1.

Training this new team was more a case of reminding each other what our vision, values and practices were, because this team was already Sorted. We tried to listen to the young adult volunteers as they shared what it had been like for them a few years earlier coming to us as younger teens. We reminded one another that today's younger teens will be different and we must listen, observe, build relationships and not rely on past experience alone.

We spent three weeks doing training as opposed to the six months needed for bringing a team together who had never done Sorted or worked together before. Sorted 3 began in November 2012 and quickly grew as Damien met people on the school playground who then came to a Friday-night session.

Reproduction – why bother?

Mike Moynagh argues in his forthcoming book, *Church in Life*,[1] that God wants mission to happen in every sphere of life. The call is to 'make disciples of all nations' (Matthew 28.19) and the subsequent vision of God's people at the end of history is of them being gathered together from 'every nation, tribe, people and language' (Revelation 7.9). For disciples to be made in every sphere of life implies that people of different tribes, cultures, subcultures and communities will need the church to become a friend.[2] If this is a call to the whole Church, then it must be a call to reproduce church as new expressions in all communities – in local communities, online communities, niche communities, and every other community you can think of that sprawls across the planet. That's a big task! My guess is that we scale it right down to thinking about a small number of unreached communities that we might be able to reproduce church in, and then pray about whether there is one that God is putting on our heart for us to focus on.

The better a fresh expression serves one particular demographic group, the less well it will serve other groups. Once it has decided to meet at a time, in a place, in a style and with an agenda that suit a specific context, it is bound to exclude people for whom that time, place, style and agenda are inappropriate. If the fresh expression wants to reach out to some of those it currently excludes, it will need to reproduce church among them afresh. This is partly why we did Sorted 2. We began to see a small number of teens turning up at Sorted 1 from Hanson, but our location would exclude most young people from Hanson. Sorted 1 was a mile away from Hanson and too far to travel for most Hanson students. Most Hanson teens listened to the latest pop music and many played football, whereas the Sorted 1 gang listened to punk and rock and some would skateboard. Nearly all dressed differently from most Hanson young people, so there was a difference in subcultures as well as geography.

As members of a fresh expression grow in their Christian faith, they will become culturally increasingly distant to others in their context. This will happen even if their shared life is highly contextualized. This is because the gospel not only embraces culture but transforms it so that, as time goes by, the fresh expression will become more and more different from its surrounding culture. And we should want this to happen. Its agenda will be increasingly different ('Can we have a session on the Trinity?').

Members' expectations of each other (e.g. behaviour) will be different. The style of worship will make it increasingly difficult for others in the context to join in (e.g. longer periods of silence). In other words, a gap will open up between the fresh expression and its context.

We saw this situation arise when Sorted 1 moved on to a nearby estate. It was assumed that Sorted 1 teens had similar backgrounds to those living on the estate (in fact some from Sorted 1 came from this estate) but we hadn't realized how much several years of being together had moulded Sorted 1 into the fresh expression they had become. It just didn't work when new groups of young people from the estate wanted to join us. The new young people brought the same behavioural issues that Sorted 1 had experienced four years earlier but the Sorted 1 teens didn't want to go backwards, they needed space to chat, be quiet, discuss faith and life.

The answer was not to struggle unsuccessfully to be relevant to the surrounding culture but to start a new expression of church. Some of the frustration with the situation led to a desire for a new fresh expression to reach younger teens. When this did happen in the form of Sorted 3, as we saw, some team members came from Sorted 1 as indigenous leaders wanting to reach out to others.

Reproduction – when, where and who?

When?

I believe God's timing is vital. Evangelism is seeing what God is doing and joining in. God knows when it's the right time to reproduce, both for us and for the people being reached. He knows when we are ready and when they are ready.

The story above shows I wasn't expecting reproduction when God wanted us to start Sorted 2, but his timing was right. A few years later, I wanted us to begin Sorted 3, but I was too early. We had to wait for a pioneer to join us, and the team were only ready to begin shortly before Damien Hine arrived.

If we'd worked according to my timetable, it wouldn't have been sustainable, the team might have become discouraged and this could have put them off trying again. So we waited until both the pioneer and the team were in place and ready.

- Is the Spirit's guidance clear? Spiritual gifts, careful observation of the circumstances and use of reason can aid discernment.
- Is there a suitable pioneer and team in place? Have they had suitable training?
- Is there a suitable leader and team to keep leading the parent church?
- Are there significant stumbling blocks to overcome before reproduction can begin?

Timing is often hard to judge. For example, you may have seven team members and be hoping for ten. Do you wait for the tenth to arrive or begin with seven? If everything else is ready, it's probably best to get started, but if other things aren't ready you might wait. Clearly, four members are too few; it will never be perfect but there needs to be enough resource to begin.

Where?

If you reproduce in the same locality as the parent church, can local people from the parent church (plus others from local churches) become the new planting team? It's important to include both mature Christians and team members who can relate to those you're trying to reach. When we began Sorted 3, our team was a mix of older mature Christians who had planted Sorted 1 a few years earlier and indigenous young Christian adults from Sorted 1. The mature ones brought wisdom and reliability while the young ones brought understanding of those we were going to reach and were much closer to their age.

This mix of both the mature and the indigenous works well for Sorted. It could well work for you.

If you reproduce in a nearby area to the parent church, do you have people who can travel to form a planting team or do you need to work with local churches to form a new team, as we did when starting Sorted 2? Or is a mix possible? A mix is good as it combines the experience of those who've done it before with those who have local knowledge.

If you reproduce many miles away from the parent church, can you send a pioneer or several people to live in the area? If not, can you build links between the new planting team and the parent church so that mutual support and learning can happen? Why not do both?

Where is God calling you to plant? How will reproducing bring in the kingdom of God for new people so that lives are transformed? How might the gospel be contextualized for these people? Is there other Christian work already fulfilling this need – can you complement each other or not? How supportive are local churches? Reflection and discussion around these questions can help the team to think clearly and plan in a focused yet flexible way. Don't worry if you can't answer all the questions when you begin; some may be answered later on and that's OK.

Who?

Here are three ways to work out who will pioneer when reproducing:[3]

1 Jesus trained his disciples for three years and then sent them to pioneer. Jesus pioneered with the disciples during those years before he left them to do it without him. One option is to appoint a trainee to pioneer when reproducing. Nick came from Ghana to train with Sorted as a Church Army trainee. Nick and I pioneered Sorted 2 together before he then went to South London to pioneer a youth church called TYM using the Sorted model.

There will need to be careful consideration of what training needs are required for a trainee. We were fortunate that Church Army provided excellent training in pioneering for Nick and yet there is no substitute for pioneering something new while training alongside someone who has done it before.

2 St Paul set up a new church, quickly appointed church elders, and then left them in charge so that he could pioneer elsewhere. We followed this example when I left Sorted 1, leaving my wife Tracy as team leader so that I could begin pioneering Sorted 2.

3 Church history is full of examples of pioneers being sent many miles to lead a team that will pioneer a new church. Sorted 3 began when Damien Hine moved to Bradford, forming a planting team made up of indigenous Sorted 1 young adults plus older adults. Tracy and I mentored Damien in this role.

Whichever option or mix of options you choose (it might be different from the three above), it's important that the person is gifted in pioneering, gets the DNA of your church and its vision, and is suitable for the context. One pioneer was hoping to pioneer among young people and young adults but it became clear that his gifting was primarily with young people, so that is where we encouraged him to pioneer. Moynagh asks: is the pioneer led by the Spirit, can he or she communicate the gospel contextually, with a good understanding of the Bible, possessing leadership ability and sent with ongoing support?[4] These are important qualities for any pioneer.

Reproduction – how to do it?

Moynagh outlines seven important factors that can help to make reproducing churches sustainable.

1 Encountering Jesus

Health and life come into the church as we encounter Jesus. Jesus must be the centre of a church's life so that it reproduces as he initiates and leads. A revival of faith in Jesus will bring the life of Jesus into a church, better enabling it to reproduce. It's no surprise that many church-planting movements have been born out of revival or renewal movements, such as the Methodists under John Wesley or modern-day Vineyard churches under John Wimber.

Prayer groups can help keep a steady flow of intercession and petition towards God so that our plans and attempts to reproduce are rooted and birthed in prayer and encountering Jesus. Yet prayer and dependence on God shouldn't replace the hard work of planning and organizing. We need planning and prayer, not one or the other.

Prayer can provide the space for God to speak and guide us so that we reproduce in his timing, blessing, strength and gifting. Pioneers need to make space to retreat and keep a close spiritual walk with God so that what they do will advance the kingdom of God. They need the prayer support of others interceding behind the scenes.

2 Intentionality

A married couple expecting their first child will choose a house with enough bedrooms for them and their baby. They may buy a car or a tent for camping holidays with new arrivals in mind. No one would buy a Robin Reliant to take the family camping if they were expecting triplets!

If we believe the church is designed to reproduce, then it makes sense to pioneer with this in mind. In Sorted, we've intentionally tried to raise up leaders with reproduction in mind. New leaders can help take over the leading of existing groups or lead new groups as we reproduce.

If we're intentional about reproducing, our use of buildings tends to become more flexible. Some building projects consume so much time and energy for so many years that you have to wonder if a church's central vision is their building rather than Jesus' mission to the lost. I'm not saying that we don't need a good use of buildings, or that this won't take investment, but if our vision is to reproduce then it will influence where we invest our limited time, energy and resources. We can't do everything and often we're better to use community facilities or share with another church so we can focus our energies on reproducing the church.

Buildings blind our vision if we only imagine growth within their framework – whether it's numbers we can squeeze into a service or whether the building is unavailable for mission as dictated by the church diary! Sometimes I'm tempted to think that the number-one fan and promoter of church buildings is Lucifer – 'Let's keep these Christians focused only on filling these seats as this will distract them from looking outside the building to the thousands that their master wants to reach' – to imagine a scene from C. S. Lewis's *Screwtape Letters*.

Let's see buildings as servants not masters. Which buildings are available that might serve God's vision? Tracy had to convince her PCC to focus on mission first and buildings second. The church had declined for years and desperately needed to grow. The temptation was to put all the energy into raising funds to get the old church roof fixed rather than use the church hall as a facility while investing energy in mission. Growing the church would most likely bring people along who could help with the roof later. They chose to invest in mission and found that the money came in to get the roof fixed anyway. I've also known small, declining churches put so much energy into renovation that virtually no one was left in the church by the time the building was complete and so it had to be sold!

3 Everything is reproducible

Reproduction focuses us on doing things simply so they can be easily taught to others and made as reproducible as possible. For example, I used to think our schools work would involve lots of Christian Unions with in-depth Christian teaching and assemblies. As Sorted developed, I realized our schools work needed to serve many young people, not the few who are likely to attend an in-depth CU session.

Our schools work became simpler, more relational and could be done through either detached work in a canteen or playground, or through a lunch club in a classroom through Jenga, Connect 4 or other simple games requiring zero preparation. This allows the youth worker to focus on relationship-building with many young people as we love and serve both the young people and the school. It also means we can adapt to the school playground, canteen or classroom, depending on where the school allows us to be. It avoids confrontation with a secular school over our Christian teaching because we don't do much in school.

Our emphasis on loving and serving means we are helping the school care and nurture often vulnerable young people, so this becomes a win–win relationship with the school they are likely to want us to be in the school long term. Most importantly, it enables us to build the relationships that bring a continual flow of young people into Sorted. We can then do the in-depth Christian teaching in our small groups or worship service. This makes our schools work simple, easy for a relational youth worker, adaptable, attractive for any school and reproducible. An outreach approach in pubs, nightclubs, cafes or gyms might consider a similar approach that is easy to reproduce.

Vision, values, teaching, practical ways to run sessions and many other things can be made simpler, teachable and repro-ducible if we keep asking ourselves – what are the key underly-ing principles that are working? How can I do this with others? How can I pass this on for someone else to do? Keeping the principle in focus but involving others gets us to the nitty gritty of what is required, whereas working alone we can tend to over-complicate things.

4 Mentoring

Please see the section on mentoring in Chapter 7.

5 Growth through networks

I've described above how Sorted seeks to become a regular part of a school community through loving and serving in a school. As we become part of the school set-up, we can then slowly develop another community from our presence within the school community. If we want to reproduce, the obvious question to ask is, 'Where is there a school we can love and serve?'

Who are you reaching? Are they part of an obvious network such as a gym, cafe or pub? Are they part of an informal network or a neighbourhood? Are there natural people of peace in these networks or neighbourhoods? If the answer to any of these questions is yes, we can start to dream how another church might be planted in one of these networks or neighbourhoods using a reproducible pattern.

6 Contextual

Did you ever see the Clone Army in the Star Wars films? Reproduction isn't about creating a set of clones. Nor are we trying to sell an IKEA-style pre-packaged flat-pack way of doing church with ten simple instructions! We want to partner with the Spirit to reproduce baby churches that share the same DNA as their parents but are unique individual creations of the Spirit as he interacts in new people and creates something fresh, new and relevant in that context.

Anyone attempting to reproduce will have a wealth of experience, learning and insight from having pioneered first time round. This enables you to see several steps ahead, identify how to deal with problems much quicker, understand what's important and what isn't. You've already travelled the journey once before, so you know what's just around the corner!

However, the danger is *over-relying* on that experience and not asking as many questions of the new context. It's like driving on a journey you've done before but getting lost on the way because a road has changed since the last time you travelled that route. Pioneers need to download the latest map and keep asking questions of the context, the new people and the new team as they go. Put simply – we need to keep our eyes and ears open and our brains switched on. First time round, the difficulty of the task forces us to continually reflect and think. Second time round, we need to be disciplined to keep reflecting and thinking.

Reproducing with a team can prevent blind spots. Once or twice, Tracy visited Sorted 2 and gave me some challenging feedback about things we weren't doing that she thought were part of the DNA of Sorted. I didn't agree with everything she said but it was certainly thought-provoking. As new leaders lead different parts of Sorted, I've spent time visiting, reviewing, reflecting and feeding back to them what is in our DNA and what isn't, focusing on vision and practical solutions.

7 Remaining missional

Being a church leader is hard work. 'Tell me something I didn't already know!' you might say. Although the daily toil of people problems, preparing talks, setting up equipment and running meetings is hard, it's important not to allow this stuff to cloud your vision or the vision of your people so that we grow inward-looking, overwhelmed and unable to look out beyond our little community. How do you rise up and see things from God's viewpoint – thousands of people living without Jesus in their lives – keeping the dream of mission and reproduction alive in our hearts?

It boils down to two things – walking humbly with God and keeping the vision alive. Walking humbly with God keeps us in step with the Spirit. Our spiritual antenna rises when we know something is out of sync if we've allowed things to cloud our outlook. This can happen a lot, but it should draw us back to prayer and seeking God afresh because something isn't quite right. Leaders need to keep communicating the vision afresh before the people. Fresh vision will keep us inspired; it will highlight the gaps in our work and moves us to prayer and to work out practical steps of how to go forward.

Our church council and our volunteer team meetings begin with a welcome and worship before swiftly focusing on the vision. I often ask the team, 'What is the vision?', or remind them of the vision in one or two sentences. We might share good news stories of how we are moving towards the vision, before focusing on the problems and challenges that need prayer and practical solutions. We might discuss how close we are to the vision and how far away we are. I might present an analysis of where I think we are and a simple strategy of what I think we should do next. The team will then discuss it and have their say (this is good to do when moving into a new stage). We then discuss other items of the agenda.

- Ask your team – what is our vision? Can you summarize it in one or two sentences?
- Discuss with the team – in what ways are we close to the vision? In what ways are we away from the vision?
- Share where you think the church is at and a plan for the next step, but allow others to disagree, offer suggestions and shape the next step with you.
- Always pray and plan practically how you can action the next part of the vision together.

Thirst Too[5] – by Sue Butler

Thirst meets in St Philip's School, Romsey Town, Cambridge. Sue Butler tells how members of Thirst helped to form a second community in the area, Thirst Too.

'As new members of our Thirst community became bolder in sharing their often new-found faith they began reaching out to others they know in the local community of Romsey Town, which is generally the "town" rather than "gown" part of Cambridge.

About a year ago, the women at Thirst were discussing how they would like their families and friends to experience what they do – through their relationship with God and each other. We still meet every Friday at school, as well as Tuesdays for prayer and Bible studies, but many of those they were trying to reach wouldn't have been able to make it to St Philip's for Thirst. As a result, we decided to find a suitable time and convenient setting for Thirst Too – a setting where these families and friends would feel comfortable.

For various reasons, the school was not an option as a venue so we approached Romsey Mill, a Christian charity sympathetic to our vision which had sufficient space.

Thirst Too now meets there once a month on Saturdays from 5pm to 7pm and whole families are invited. These still tend to be drawn from St Philip's School, and they often bring friends with them as well. So far, we average about 55 people attending.'

Notes

1 Michael Moynagh, *Church in Life*, London: SCM Press, forthcoming 2017.
2 See Michael Moynagh, *Being Church, Doing Life: Creating Gospel Communities where Life Happens*, Oxford: Monarch, 2014, ch. 1.
3 Michael Moynagh, *Church for Every Context*, London: SCM Press, 2012, p. 412.
4 Moynagh, *Church for Every Context*, p. 415.
5 Story by Sue Butler: www.freshexpressions.org.uk/stories/thirsttoo.

Baptism, communion and Bishops' Mission Orders – how do we introduce them among people of no church background?

Culture vulture or traditionalist?

Culture is complex! When I was young, I was taught that each country had its own culture and ways of doing things. I've since come to realize that even within one age group of one country, there can be several subcultures plus national culture influencing a person's identity. This melting pot of different cultural mixes will influence a person's lifestyle and way of being human, often making a unique blend.

Since Jesus went back to heaven, his people have spread throughout every continent and influenced history over 2,000 years. During that time, Jesus has been guiding and speaking to his Church. Many of the Church's practices have developed because his people were guided by him within their own time and culture.

Some of these practices become living traditions. Many have enormous value today, such as Ignatian meditations, the Apostles' Creed or communion liturgies. But living traditions also present a big challenge too. Because most traditions were birthed in specific cultures at different times over the last 2,000 years, we can't just pick them off the shelf and assume they will work with those we minister to. This leaves us with a couple of questions:

- How can we make use of living traditions today when planting churches within specific subcultures?
- How do we stay faithful to the Church's living traditions while also being faithful to inculturating the gospel so that newly planted churches will truly be 'fresh' expressions of church?

Do the Church's living traditions bring life today?

This chapter will explore baptism and communion as two key living traditions that are rooted in the life and teaching of Jesus. It will then explore the use of liturgy – another very important living tradition. Finally, we will explore Bishops' Mission Orders, a useful tool set up by the Anglican Church but with relevance to others.

Baptism

It was a dark winter night, our young people were ready, but a new group had just arrived to watch what was about to happen, having heard rumours on the grapevine!

Being slightly agitated, I checked my watch again and looked to the car park as I waited for the Bishop to arrive. I got on well with the Bishop and he was very pro-youth work but it was still a nervy moment when a guest from the wider Church came to Sorted in those days.

I tried to suppress the fear that it would all go wrong. Our worship services still had the potential to descend into complete chaos! Most weeks were fine, the chaos did now seem behind us, but you could never be certain. I prayed again that the Bishop (whom I guessed would be used to church kids who were better behaved) wouldn't leave later that night thinking Sorted was a waste of time.

I'd told the young people, 'We need to show him Sorted at its best because not everyone in our diocese thinks a youth church is a good thing' (this was true). I spoke to the young people honestly so I might get the best out of them.

Panic! The new group had sat down, others then joined them, and our young people were getting wound up by the thought of this new group being entertained watching them get baptized. I'd been chatting to the Bishop, discussing the format of the service and missed what was happening.

Jenny suddenly rushed up to me and said none of our young people were going to be baptized if the new group stayed! One of our guys was already walking out of the door. So, quickly, while the Bishop was distracted robing up, I tried to talk to our young people. It was no good; they were convinced the others were just here for the show.

I rushed to the new group, explained that this was a special occasion for regulars only, but they would be very welcome next week – fortunately they left without kicking up a fuss. I then sprinted up the path and managed to catch up with two of our lads on their way home. Gradually our young people started to relax and we managed to get everyone back on track, just as the Bishop finished robing up and was ready to begin.

As it turned out, the baptisms went well, the young people did well and the Bishop was great with them! Travelling through the formality, ritual and symbolism of the baptism service with a bishop leading, the young people were now experiencing and starting to understand one of the most important living traditions of Jesus' Church. Through the Bishop, they were also getting an understanding of Jesus' Church and the fact they were part of something much bigger and wider than Sorted alone. They enjoyed the ritual and the occasion, and sensed their baptism was an important spiritual moment.

Some young people from broken homes, and especially those who live in the care system, take the idea of Godparents very seriously (even if they are aged 17 and so technically they have sponsors not Godparents). They mention their Godparents far more than I've ever heard Godparents mentioned anywhere else. This is probably because Sorted really is family for those who don't have a family and their Godparents play a particular role, giving them a sense of identity.

Baptism – tribal dimensions within postmodern subcultures

Vincent Donovan worked as a Catholic priest among the Masai tribes in East Africa. After several weeks of explaining the Christian faith to a tribe, the elders would be asked if the tribe wanted to be baptized. When an elder said yes, he was speaking on behalf of his whole tribe not just himself.

When Donovan protested that a certain man shouldn't be baptized because he hadn't been around during the teaching sessions, the tribe elder insisted the man had been doing essential work on behalf of the tribe and others had sat in on the teaching sessions on the man's behalf!

'He [the Masai man] agreed to take this step [baptism] only within the framework of his community, with his community, bringing his relations and relationships with him', wrote Donovan.[1] This can seem strange in western society where so much emphasis is placed on the individual but it was natural to the Masai.

In Sorted, a young person of peace will often find faith and then brings his or her friends to discover faith. These young people will learn about God together and step forward into Christian faith together. This has been of huge importance for most young people.

For a young person growing up in church, their family life and church family life will include the Christian faith and so getting baptized or confirmed is a natural way to go even though it's a decision about relationship with Christ. This happens within a family or church family context.

It's rare for a young person with no experience of Christianity in the home or the Church to come to faith and baptism as an individual. Among those who belong to a teen tribe or solid group of peers, it's even rarer unless the whole tribe find faith together. This is because they would have to stand outside their community and often go against the traditions of the teen tribe to come to faith as an individual. I spent years bringing individual young people of zero Christian background to become Christians only to see them drop off the radar soon after due to the influence of their peers. I came to realize the whole group had to come to faith.

Getting baptized at Sorted was both a decision for Christ and a decision to keep travelling within their tribe. The young people chose to join the Church as a tribe not as individuals. In many postmodern subcultures, the tribal element is important for us to understand. The same principles may hold true with surfers in their twenties or even climbers in their thirties – taking the group forward into baptism together might be a good way to go.

Much evangelism to young people has focused on drawing them into a faith community while ignoring the fact the young person is already part of a teen tribe community. Our drawing them into one community can put strain on their place within their teen tribe. We're only likely to reach generations of teens, twenties and postmodern thirties if we can grasp the community element of teen tribes and many other subcultures of adults. Starting where they are at, working within their existing tribes, incarnating the gospel and taking them as a group on a faith journey towards baptism is the only way of working with the grain of their community rather than against the grain by unintentionally pulling individuals away from their pre-existing tribes.

Communion

We tried to make sure our worship was participative, interactive and bite-sized (see the end of Chapter 8). Someone did a teaching based on 'Taste and see the LORD is good' (Psalm 34.8), giving out pieces of fruit, honey and other food, making the point that we experience God, his word and Spirit like sweet honey or tasty fruit. Young people really connected to this.

A few weeks later, after showing a DVD clip of the Last Supper and explaining briefly why Jesus died for our sins, bread and blackcurrant juice were placed in bowls on low tables near the front of our worship area. Young people gave out pieces of bread and sips of juice during a quiet time. It was participative, interactive, short and simple, yet in line with the command of Jesus, who said, 'do this (break bread and sip wine together) in remembrance of me' (1 Corinthians 11.24). Once again, young people connected!

Our early symbolic efforts at doing communion helped young people to remember Jesus and understand a little more of the cross. As time went by, we began to experiment with using liturgy and moving towards 'official' communion with liturgy.

When the Bishop first baptized our young people, he allowed me to reword some of the service so that the language would be more accessible to young people. Many hadn't done well in school and would struggle with 'wordy' Anglican liturgy so we tried to simplify it, while staying true to the text.

As time went by, Tracy was ordained priest and would explain some bits of the liturgy to our older young people, being careful not to overburden them. As young people have been confirmed, we're now able to celebrate communion with them and use the liturgy creatively so that it becomes an aid to enhance our remembrance and worship of Jesus not hinder it!

We've celebrated communion with different forms of the official liturgy, as well as broken bread informally. Young people find something mysterious, ethereal and awesome about communion with its ritual and symbolism. It speaks of a God who is mighty, who humbled himself to death on a cross for our sins.

Introducing communion gradually, beginning with symbolic sharing of bread and wine to remember Jesus, then moving towards full-blown liturgical communion, should be done sensitively. It's better to go at the pace of the new people, making sure they understand what's happening and why, involving them in the process and being ready to take two steps forward and one back if need be. Communion is more likely to be full of spiritual meaning when we introduce it as a process with conversations throughout the process rather than thrust full-blown communion on them when they don't yet have a clue what's going on.

Communion – inclusive or exclusive

Murray outlines three different approaches to communion that range from being very inclusive of both believers and non-believers to being exclusively limited to believers only.[2] An 'open set' approach might happen in 'table churches' and often the words of institution are left out so that communion is open to all. A 'centred set' approach is similar, yet with the key difference of a core community of believers whom others are moving towards. Third, a 'bounded set' approach takes the view that communion is only for the baptized or confirmed.

My concern in the early days of Sorted was that we were working with teen tribes and so community already existed in some form. If young people were to be baptized and confirmed, how could we avoid an 'exclusive situation' where we unintentionally broke up their community by separating the confirmed from the unconfirmed? Sorted was inclusive in its approach. Our early prayers were about 'becoming aware of the God who is with all of us, connecting to this God who loves each one'. Our focus was about connection – with each other and with God. The challenge of discipleship then becomes 'staying connected to God 24/7' via prayer, Bible reading, treating others like Jesus would and community worship. Words that spoke of us being a family with God in the centre, being on an adventure of faith together or stepping into the new things God has for us, all worked with the grain of community not against it. Most things that promoted exclusivity and divided people from one another (albeit unintentionally) didn't have a long shelf life.

For Sorted, the 'bounded set' approach wouldn't work as it might be too divisive, so we ruled it out. In many contexts, the 'open set' might work and be an effective evangelistic tool. There is so much at the heart of communion about community life, such as:

- sharing together in one bread
- partaking together in the life of God

- love for one another modelled supremely by Jesus' self-sacrificial love
- the foretaste of heaven – the destination of the shared journey of faith
- grieving the loss of a community leader
- the hope of new life together in the future.

The 'open set' approach could engage with many postmodern communities, especially those who are open to the spiritual and to ritual. This might happen with a church meeting in a pub or cafe.

The 'centred set' approach works well in a new church based on the 'serving first' stages of mission, such as community gatherings, small groups and a worship service. The worship service can become the core of the Christian community and take communion. As others are drawn through the stages and into worship, they are likely to be able to understand communion and participate at a spiritual level.

A 'centred set' approach can involve the regular worshippers organizing and setting up 'communion' for new people as they become ready to attend. Everyone ready to join in worship is valued and included. The act of partaking in bread and wine is modelled by the core community and yet others are affirmed of God's love and become aware of Jesus' death on their behalf, the ransom paid to set them free and bring new life. Those not wanting to take communion are simply encouraged to be respectful and silent while this happens.

Liturgy

Liturgy is a loaded word among many Christians. If I say I like liturgy to some evangelical charismatic friends, they will no doubt disapprove, thinking liturgy quenches the Spirit, ties us up in the red tape of traditionalism or holds us back because it represents religion not faith.

At the other end of the spectrum, if I mention that I question or doubt the value of a piece of official church liturgy in the presence of some Anglo-Catholic friends, they will suspect I don't lead a real church! What do we do with this baggage, especially when we're trying to find a way forward for a new church? How do we find a way of being loyal to the living tradition of liturgy while also being contextual?

On the wall in the library of the Bible college, there was a big portrait of Church Army's founder, Wilson Carlile. On my first day as we were being shown round, a tutor explained that some students had drawn or written comments on stick-on notes and pinned them to the portrait. These words or pictures weren't offensive or aimed at belittling the man in the portrait; they were humorous reflections of college life posted on to his portrait. They actually made me think a bit more about who Wilson Carlile was, what he stood for and what he might make of us lot continuing his organization. They connected our life in college today to him and his life.

Perhaps we can use liturgy like the college students above. If we can be creative with liturgy, have fun and play around with it, write our own versions and draw or paint it, we stand a chance of connecting it to our own community lives. By doing this, we are investing it with meaning from our lives and Scripture. If we can help people connect liturgy with real life, as we often do with the psalms, then it's likely to make us reflect more deeply about Jesus, the Trinity and the Church.

'Liturgy should be truly inculturated', reported an international gathering of liturgists in York in 1989.[3] Worship, and therefore liturgy, should be truly catholic if it is to include and embrace people from all cultures. If it can only exist in a single cultural form, can it really represent the faith of peoples from every tribe, culture and nation? Yet if it is to become truly catholic, how can this happen unless we're allowed to play with it and be creative with it so that it connects to our lives today?

Whether it's rewording a baptism or communion service, writing your own liturgy that is consistent with the Church's official liturgies, or mixing both, liturgy should be alive not dead! At Sorted, we've reworded official services, used official liturgy as it is and written our own prayers of confession and spoken together a statement of who we are – 'We are Sorted youth church, we have come together to worship God . . .'

'A form or formulary according to which public religious worship, especially Christian worship, is conducted.'[4] If we use this *Oxford Dictionary* definition, then surely liturgy isn't limited to creeds and official liturgies. It should see the Church's official liturgies as the foundation stone on which other liturgies can be built. For example, I might write a poem about Jesus, but my words should be consistent with the truth of the Apostles' Creed.

If liturgy is to truly connect context and tradition then it should include favourite songs or Bible passages of a church, if they carry special meaning. What about images, pictures or spiritual exercises? Perhaps it's the meaning behind these things that determines whether or not they can be part of our liturgy. If a church finds a favourite song full of meaning, then this might become part of that church's liturgy for a season. If a piece of artwork is invested in meaning for the congregation, could this become part of the liturgy for a season, perhaps coupled with some words?

If you want to introduce liturgy, consider the following:

1 Value liturgy as a gift from God, part of the Church's living tradition.
2 Ask which liturgies might aid, challenge or inspire the worship of a particular new church.
3 Is there liturgy that needs rewording to make it accessible? If I do reword liturgy, can I get someone to double-check it so that I'm making sure it is consistent with the original wording?
4 Are there songs, Bible passages or specific prayers that may become regular parts of our worship for a season? Many congregations find themselves really able to worship with a certain song because it has meaning.
5 How can we encourage people to be creative – draw, write, paint or make things creatively – that might become part of our liturgy for a season? How do we decide what becomes part of our liturgy and what doesn't? Is a group needed to

pray and decide so that someone's pet project doesn't keep taking centre stage?

6 How do we get a good balance between use of what I have called 'official liturgy', such as creeds, baptism and communion prayers, alongside liturgy that is reworded or creative?

7 Within my denomination or network, when am I allowed to be creative and when do I need to stick with official liturgies?

Bishop's Mission Order (BMO)

Depending on which denomination or church network we are part of, if we start a new church it often feels like we are the new kid on the block. Before we even begin, for some of us it can feel like we've got to prove our worth time and time again.

Fresh expressions or similar churches are sometimes viewed as competition or the latest church fad. We won't be supported and understood by everyone. Expectations will vary among local church leaders and their congregations, sometimes making it difficult when you're starting out.

These factors taken together can make us feel like the odds are stacked against us. In many places, this won't be a problem, but in others it can seem very hard to get to where God wants us to be. One thing that can really help us is if our denomination or network creates a tool that deals with all the expectations, potential conflict and confusion over how we relate to existing churches so that God's mission can be helped not hindered.

A BMO is one such tool that has been designed by the Anglican Church. In principle, something similar could be used in any denomination or network. A BMO is a licence from the bishop of a diocese for a fresh expression of church to exist within a specific geographical area and with a specified purpose. Sorted exists across six parishes with a particular focus of working with young people and their networks outside existing churches. It complements the work of parish churches who work with young people who've either grown up in church or who mostly attend church because they have friends in church. Other BMOs will specify the purpose of the new church and how it relates to existing local churches.

Bishop's Mission Order – is it for us?

'Is it a church or are the young people going to join us on a Sunday morning when they hit 18?' asked a local churchwarden.

'Where does Sorted fit into the local churches?' asked a local vicar.

'Who will administer communion?' asked someone else.

During the first six years of our existence, we were continually asked these kinds of questions. Some would ask out of pure concern that we find the best way of helping new Christian young people continue their discipleship into adulthood, while a minority just didn't believe Sorted should be a new church.

These questions simply would not go away. I attended management meetings two or three times a year. The same questions would be asked, often by a couple of older priests who couldn't see Sorted as anything other than a youth project whose young people should be fed into 'real' church on a Sunday morning by age 18.

It annoyed me that they never asked: What are you learning about mission to young people? What do young people make of the gospel? What has Jesus been saying to you lately? They seemed only to ask the churchy questions but not the God questions. Over time, some of the priests had a conversion experience and began to view Sorted as a church, but others didn't.

Yet many of us in the management group learnt together how Sorted was to develop as a church and we began to see how discipleship could be continued with groups for those 18+ and those who were becoming young parents. We began to see how the work of Sorted really did complement the work of the existing churches and we began to administer communion, as I will explain below.

During these years, there were also really encouraging times, moments of real insight and learning through debating the tough questions. It was also a battle for survival and identity. I had many sleepless nights both before and after these management group meetings as my head pounded with thinking about what would be asked and how I would answer.

On one level, it was upsetting that we had to endure a level of scrutiny and questioning by a couple of priests who themselves would never be subject to that level of questioning and inquisition in their role as parish priests. It bothered Tracy because she worked part time with Sorted and part time as a parish priest; she always felt Sorted had to prove itself every step of the way, whereas she never experienced this in the parish to the same degree.

However, we weren't just pioneering a youth church practically with young people; we were also pioneering in the sense that we were travelling into new territory for the diocese, and so much of the intense questioning reflected the need to keep us accountable, safe and on track. The diocese realized we were pioneering in a complex context and so working out mission strategy and priorities wasn't straightforward. There were people with expertise and experience of both fresh expressions and youth work at our management meetings, and their input was invaluable for Sorted.

Getting a BMO could feel like a test of diplomacy to rival the Iran nuclear deal of 2015! Most church leaders were in favour, but one or two had serious objections. One church leader was scared the BMO might give us a free reign to do whatever in his parish (the BMO gives specific permissions not a free-for-all). Another was scared that our volunteers (from a church he had taken over) would give financially to Sorted and not the parish church. The second issue was quickly resolved after I visited him to explain Sorted didn't want to divert giving from the parish to ourselves.

Getting a BMO was a huge step forward for Sorted. It was like getting a birth certificate or being adopted into a family. Our identity as a youth church was now official! Many of the unhelpful old questions dried up and it was like a new beginning at the management meetings, which still weren't easy, but at least our new identity within the diocese gave us stability, support and a new future where we belonged in a way that we hadn't before.

'How are you going to do a PCC meeting with your teenagers?' asked a Christian leader at a conference. Many people wondered how we'd cope with church council meetings, finding churchwardens and Annual General Meetings with teenagers. As it happened, these things became opportunities not problems.

Sorted had begun in the POD in April 2005. As AGMs had to be done in March or April, we decided to hold a Sorted Birthday Party each year both to celebrate our birthday and to hold the AGM. Each year the birthday party begins with worship, moves into a quick AGM business meeting and finishes with a party of food, drink, good music and dancing! It seems to work; the vision is shared for the next year and, although our business meeting is brief, local priests assure me we are doing everything legally.

When appointing churchwardens (much like elders or stewards in other denominations) we appoint a long-standing volunteer alongside a young adult. Simon, who has been part of Sorted since its inception, has brought reliability, stability and maturity to the role while various young adults have brought insights and the representation of their peers.

We've done team meetings with young people for years. Putting together a church council basically means a team meeting plus minutes. When we elect new members on to the church council, we encourage other young people to see them as their elected representatives who are really important as they give young people a voice and a vote.

As Sorted received a BMO, the management group became a liaison group. The new name reflected the new purpose of the group, which was to enable liaising between Sorted and existing local churches through an update on our work, space for questions and issues to be raised and sometimes for opinions to be sought out. While it was important liaison didn't slip back into management, the conversations did become increasingly positive as time went by. New church leaders moving into the area would hear about Sorted in advance and the liaison group would usually enable them to come into a group where the old questions of what Sorted is were already settled and dealt with. This made working with new leaders easier as we could focus on building a relationship of mutual respect and trust without any of the old uncertainties.

Messy Church, Wingerworth – by Jo White[5]

After deciding to have a baptism and confirmation service for people with little or no church background, they soon discovered that this would be far from straightforward! Here is an excerpt of what happened next!

'The idea took off big time – as did the questions, "Will I have to come to church on Sundays in future 'cos I work that day as my husband's at home to look after the children and so I can't do it." "Me too – I feel a fraud as I only come here and not to 'proper' church – it's just it reminds me of when I was a child and that was a terrible time for me."

The comments just kept on coming . . . "I want to get confirmed here, even though I live two hours away – I was brought up here and my family still live here, but above all these are the people who make me feel I belong." "I heard my brother's getting confirmed, so I'd love to do it with him." "I was confirmed as a kid, but I don't remember it, I wish I could do it with you." "Well I'm Catholic, but this is really my church now."

So we spoke about Communion. What should we do about the bread and wine? We've never "done" Communion before. When would you like to take it, at the confirmation service itself or shall we get together a few days later? Let's go for it! What about the kids? (In this church you have to be baptized and over seven years old.) Hence we started preparing them too!

Needless to say, everyone who came to this service did know it would be different and longer! The key pressures came from balancing the need of the Bishop to follow the "law" of the Church of England and our wish to make the service accessible and understandable for the majority of the Messy Church congregation who are either children or have none or little experience of "formal" church. How do you make such a huge formal service needing loads of preparation and "serious" thinking accessible to all of us at our different stages in our faith journeys?"

Notes

1 Vincent Donovan, *Christianity Rediscovered*, London: SCM Press, 1978, p. 69.
2 Stuart Murray in Michael Moynagh, *Church for Every Context*, London: SCM Press, 2012, p. 358.
3 1989 York Statement in Moynagh, *Church for Every Context*.
4 Oxford Dictionary: http://www.oxforddictionaries.com.
5 Story of Messy Church, Wingerworth: www.freshexpressions.org .uk/stories/allsaintswingerworth.

Finally

For more information on Bishop's Mission Orders, go to: www.fresh expressions.org.uk/resources/bmoguide.

For creative ways to do communion for different ages/contexts, go to: www.freshexpressions.org.uk/guide/worship/communion.

12

Can you make a fresh expression of church sustainable?

Do the maths!

> Surveying 57 stories of new churches since 1999 . . . 16
> founders were still in the saddle. In 21 cases, the founder was
> replaced and life continued well . . . 14 churches ceased to
> exist. In 8 of these, either the founder was not replaced or a
> poor appointment was made. In 9 of the 14 cases, the young
> church was too dependent on the founder.[1]

Do the maths! For every three churches where the founder left
and things continued well, there were two churches that went
to the wall. The sums speak for themselves – sustainability of a
new church is not a given, especially when the founder moves
on. Is it possible to increase the level of sustainability and the
likelihood of life continuing well, especially when the founder
leaves?

When the pioneer leaves . . .

'You can't leave, it'll start falling apart!' said a team member
as I shared my plan to gradually leave Sorted 1 so that I could
make time to start Sorted 2.

'But *your* relationship with the young people is key,' came
another comment.

The second statement was partly true. My relationship with many of the young people had been very important during the early stages of Sorted 1. High levels of deprivation in our locality only added to the importance of relationships and the sense of rejection that might be experienced if someone left.

But things had moved on and were now more established. The young people had a very good relationship with Tracy and their relationships with Simon and Val weren't far behind either. Despite the progress, I still worried about when would be the right time to leave and delegate leadership of the sessions. I wanted to do this in the best way possible so that life could continue well in Sorted 1.

Taking time

Timing was dictated largely by the start of Sorted 2. Responding to God's call to begin Sorted 2 forced my hand. There came a point when I simply had to step out of the Friday-night activity session at Sorted 1 and lead the team training at Sorted 2. There were no other free evenings available, as Tracy now had extra commitments due to her curacy. If the question of *when* to leave and delegate was already being answered, then the other question of *how* to delegate the sessions was still up for grabs. How could we do it as wisely and as harmlessly as possible to Sorted 1?

There are numerous stories of big youth groups falling apart with lots of young people leaving when the leader leaves. I wanted to leave well and alone! So I gradually delegated leadership of the Sorted 1 evening sessions to others over a 20-month period, making sure that each session had readjusted to the new leader before attempting to delegate the next one.

TIP 1 – If your church has different gatherings, delegate one at a time, making sure each gathering is running smoothly without you before you start to delegate the next gathering.

I handed over the Friday-night session in April 2008, and then the Monday youth worship service in October of the same year. Finally, I handed over leadership of the Tuesday-night small groups in January 2010 when a new leader had been trained and was ready.

We did it in that order (Friday, Monday and then Tuesday) partly so that I could be at Sorted 2 on Fridays, but also because we had leaders ready and able to take over on Friday and then Monday, although we had to wait a while before we had a suitable leader ready and able to step in and take over on Tuesdays.

There was always an underlying commitment to delegate and leave via a process, giving young people time to get used to someone else's leadership style, taking time to mentor a new leader, making sure the vision and values were upheld so that the transition would be as smooth as possible.

Without a doubt, delegating the Friday activity session was the scariest transition to make. We had never done this before and I knew many of the young people didn't want me to leave even though they knew there was a really good reason for me to go, such as, 'Hey, we can do Sorted again, just up the road!' In a high-deprivation context where young people saw us as surrogate parents, would Sorted 1 continue or gradually collapse?

Having Tracy to lead and Simon to co-lead the Sorted 1 Friday session was vital. Both knew the vision well, modelled the values and related well to the young people. Over a six-week period, Tracy and Simon started leading the session (with Tracy as the main leader) and I would pop in every other week. In between sessions, Tracy and I would pray and chat about each aspect of the Friday-night session and the role of the leader. We also spent time being absolutely clear about what we were trying to achieve and how best to do it. Tracy later continued this process with the existing team. I tried to share everything I knew so that Tracy would be as informed as possible. It's better that a new leader start by doing most of what has been done before by the old leader, but once they have the trust of the people then they can start to make changes, as long as its within the framework of agreed vision and values.

TIP 2 – By mentoring your successor – praying, planning and discussing the session together, looking at its vision and discussing how best to lead it – you are setting them up to succeed.

What we've since discovered during several handovers of leadership is that there is always some aspect of the leader's role that the new leader is unaware of or blind to. Tracy already knew how much time I spent just going round and chatting to all the young people each Friday, and yet it hadn't occurred to her just how important it was for a new leader to do this and provide some of the glue that made the group cohesive. To her credit, she soon learnt this role and carried it out brilliantly. When James took over this session from Tracy in 2011, the same thing happened and it took him a while to adjust to becoming a 'shepherd'. Having seen Tracy and me carry out this shepherding role, several young people helped James into this role, explaining how and why it was so important.[2]

Five months later, Tracy took over leadership at the Monday-night youth congregation. This was both an easier and more difficult transition to make. Easier because Tracy and I were virtually sharing the up-front roles by that time and Val was also heavily involved. This group related just as well to Tracy as to me. Yet a lack of adult volunteers meant that I couldn't leave quickly and so the transition took a lot longer.

In some ways, the situation of Tracy increasingly leading the service with me still there on the night helped make it a smooth leadership transition at the right pace. God provides the resources for the thing he's calling us to do, so when the resources are not there, it should cause us to explore why. It may be that we're not doing enough to find the resources, but it could also be that God is withholding them for a reason.

Same vision, different gifts

Tracy is very good at both encouraging and enabling people to find their gift and use it. As I left each session, Tracy turned this into an opportunity by saying to the young people, 'Look, Andy's been sent to do Sorted 2, that means we've got to run Sorted 1 together.' When we first started the youth congregation, Tracy had done her teaching with John as a way of mentoring him. Now Tracy was leading Fridays, she used her gifts to bring two more young people into a leadership role. Peter had seen how I had led Fridays and the way I talked to everyone and so, using the register as a way in, he joined Tracy in taking on the role of shepherding as I had done.

TIP 3 – A change of leadership is an opportunity for team members to discover their gifts, fill the pioneer's shoes and accomplish much more besides.

Tracy consolidated the team of young people, making it very clear that as a team working with her and Simon, they had to get involved, make decisions and run things. It was during this period that a young person called Joe coined the phrase 'by young people, for young people' to describe what was happening. This phrase is now well known and used to describe one of our key values.

If I was the pioneer, God now used Tracy as the settler, consolidating the progress made up to this point and building upon it. Despite the different focus of our gifts, we quickly worked out that the most important thing was to be very clear about what the vision or purpose is for each session and to be flexible in how that is worked out practically. The different gifts emphasis would spill out in the process, bringing about what God wanted in the life of Sorted at that stage of its journey. Tracy fulfilled the task Paul gave Titus, when he told him, 'The reason I left you in Crete, was that you might straighten out what was left unfinished and appoint elders in every town' (Titus 1.5).

Both as a curate in a parish working alongside a vicar and when taking over from me, Tracy was always totally loyal to the senior leader. She always spoke positively about the senior leader and the vision they worked to – I think this only helped to foster a positive culture in the places she worked as well as a 'can do' approach to life after I left Sorted 1.

THE DNA OF PIONEER MINISTRY

TIP 4 – If you replace the founder, be positive about the founder, their vision and especially about the team's ability to go forward in that vision.

Tracy is more extravert than me; she can be loud, whereas I tend to be quiet. On the surface, we appear quite different, yet the underlying vision and values remained constant, with a continued emphasis on relationships, empowerment and so on. It's so important the vision and values remain constant during the first few years after the founder leaves in a fragile church plant so that there is some stability and the people don't have too much change too soon.

TIP 5 – It's OK if the first leader after the founder has different gifts and a different personality but he or she should lead with the same purpose, vision and values as the founder.

It wasn't long before Tracy adapted a few things, but the vision, values and main thrust of Sorted stayed the same. Tracy could start making adaptations sooner than someone new to Sorted because she had established relationships and knew the DNA, whereas someone from the outside would have to take longer to earn trust and be sure they really understood the DNA.

What are you trying to sustain?

You might be tempted to answer, 'It's the new church, dummy!' But we've found that different partners have slightly different answers to this question. Your denomination or church network might be very happy that a new church exists and will be even happier if the church can keep paying its way and continue existing long term. Sustaining the status quo might be the priority to this partner. Others might prioritize numerical growth. Team members might prioritize spiritual depth, while visionaries might prioritize reproduction.

In an ideal world, we will hope all these things are sustained simultaneously, but this might be unrealistic so it's worth exploring the question, 'What are God's priorities at this moment in time?' The vine and branches metaphor in John 15 tells us that God wants to prune our work so that it becomes even more fruitful. Pruning is tough; it may mean cutting back in one area so that another can grow more quickly. Discerning God's priorities for our work means keeping the vision fresh and up to date.

The 'three selfs' model was developed in the nineteenth century.[3] It's widely used as a model to measure sustainability today. Mike Moynagh shows the limitations of the 'three selfs model – self-financing, self-governing and self-reproducing', questioning if this is the best way to measure sustainability in contextual churches or fresh expressions within the mixed economy environment of Europe or North America today.[4]

For example, it will take years before Sorted becomes self-financing by raising money through the collection plate. Most of our members are at school and many live in areas of deprivation, so while they do give financially as part of their discipleship, they won't raise significant income until many are in full-time employment. The same issue affects churches in urban priority areas where many members are on low incomes. Equally, it would be nonsense to suggest that a large, rich and healthy church that has been around for 150 years but has never reproduced is unsustainable!

Moynagh suggests four Fs as an alternative – Fruitfulness, Flow, Family and Freedom.

- **Fruitfulness** – is the new church fruitful in terms of growing closer to God, growing mature relationships in the world, wider body and within the gathering?
- **Flow** – is there a flow of people into other local churches; that is, can people switch to another church when it serves their needs better (many fresh expressions and contextual churches focus on a particular social group such as students, club culture or Saga generation)? Overlaps between churches can foster interdependence and provide options for new Christians to join other churches if their lifestyle or needs change.

- **Family** – does the new church contribute to the wider Church as it shares learning, and does it play a part in the wider Church?
- **Freedom** – does the new church have an appropriate amount of independence and responsibility for itself?

The four Fs provide helpful measures of sustainability for many in contextual churches or fresh expressions where the aim is to work in complementary relationships with existing churches. These relationships are vital so that both inherited and fresh/contextual churches learn and grow together. This makes the four Fs a helpful model for this context. However, both models have much to offer and I think there is room for other models too; perhaps a combination of models might be helpful. We will revisit these models later.

Debate around 'models of sustainability' reminds us that different partners and team members will have different priorities when it comes to measuring sustainability. So what *should* we try to sustain? The following questions may help us discern God's priorities:

- What was the *initial calling* from God that led to the creation of a new church?
- What was the *practical outworking* of the vision arising from the calling?
- Has the calling *changed or altered*? If so, what are the implications for the practical outworking of the vision today?
- *Prioritize* the activities of your church so that they are in line with today's calling and practical outworking of the vision.
- Be prepared to consider *discarding* those things that are not in line with the calling and vision.

Some youth churches deliberately feed their young people into a traditional church when teens hit 18 and find young adult work irrelevant because 90% of their young people go to university and move away (whereas 90% of our teens stay around).[5] Sustainability for such a youth church may mean prioritizing mission to young teens entering the youth church, maintaining groups that help them come to faith and finding a flow so that

18-year-olds can transition into a university Christian Union or traditional church.

Yet Sorted works mainly with those of no church background, so we knew the majority wouldn't transition into traditional church at 18. Despite a tiny number of our young people finding a home in a traditional church at 18, most find the culture gap too big to jump over and won't make that transition. We sensed God wanted us to create young adult church instead. For Sorted in the north Bradford context, sustainability means prioritizing both developing church with people as they become young adults while maintaining mission to teens and youth church. However, doing Sorted in a different context could theoretically mean that, at 18, young people mostly transition to university. The important point is that sustainability will mean different priorities in different contexts.

> *Question – Sustainability will look different in different contexts. Can you identify how your context will influence what you try to sustain?*

MAKING IT SUSTAINABLE – PART I

Three selfs

1 Self-financing

When new people start attending church, it's normal not to ask them to contribute financially until they've become Christians. This is so they don't feel the church is only after their money. Giving happens later on as a way of showing our love for Jesus.

However, giving can begin much earlier too. If we're trying to model Christian values such as forgiveness or prayer with both Christians and 'not yet' Christians in a cafe church or through a spirituality course, why not do the same with giving?

We've found it easier to inject the right DNA into a new church at the beginning of its journey rather than wait until much later on. Waiting until much later increases the danger of new people becoming church consumers rather than being a part of the team. Encouraging 'not yet' Christians to give financially to support the new church enables them to make a contribution and get involved.

A new church struggling with low giving because they exist in an area of poverty or deprivation may consider becoming a charity, with a group of directors and a constitution. This will enable them to apply to many trust funds for grants, which they're more likely to gain if they have charitable trust status. It's a complex process and advice should be sought from others who've already done this, perhaps from within your denomination or church network. Check out www.charitycommission.gov.uk for more information.

Starting a new church with a low-cost approach will help. Raising lay leaders and sharing the tasks of leadership can reduce the need for paid staff. Renting or using other churches' buildings or community facilities can minimize the cost of buildings. Gathering resources from other local churches or pooling together with new members can reduce the money needed to be spent on new resources. All these things will be easier in suburban or middle-class areas where new members are increasingly likely to have the skills and abilities to take part in leadership. Those working in areas of high deprivation may find that training lay leaders takes longer. There may be more need for trained, paid staff in such areas, which makes dependence on outside funding harder to avoid.

2 Self-governing

Self-governance empowers new members of a church to determine its direction and future through prayer, discussion and making decisions together. Early on in Sorted, it quickly became apparent that the local Anglican church council wouldn't be a good group to make decisions for Sorted because many of its members didn't understand our vision or context. Our initial pioneering team took advice from a variety of people with expertise in youth work and fresh expressions. It quickly became clear that we needed to be able to steer our own ship while being accountable. A suitable process to do this came to us in 2010 through a Bishop's Mission Order (see Chapter 11 to find out how a BMO provides self-governance and accountability).

Right from the beginning, we aimed to foster 'self-governance' simply by increasing ownership among the new people through teamwork. Each gathering or group in the church can include some level of teamwork. Teams meeting for a couple of hours or teams meeting for a few minutes before a session can discuss how to raise finance, implement vision or how to find solutions to problems. As we involve others in this teamwork, we are creating a culture where self-governance is being learnt, practised and modelled.

A new church might only gain 'true' self-governance when this is granted formally by people more senior in the denomination or church network through a legal licence. In many lay-led fresh expressions, it may never be formally granted but simply assumed from the beginning that the new church will self-govern. Whatever your situation, introduce teamwork early on so that the church can learn self-governance. The better the teamwork, the more new members partake in decisions about finance, vision and problem-solving, and the more likely those in authority will recognize that a new church is ready to be formally granted self-governance. Good teamwork will make it easier for the new church to argue the case for its own 'true' self-governance, should it need too.

3 Self-reproducing

Please see Chapter 10 on reproduction.

Four Fs

1 Fruitfulness

Jesus promised that we would bear much fruit if we remain in him (John 15.7). Moynagh suggests that we measure fruitfulness by asking, 'Is the new church fruitful in terms of growing closer to God, growing mature relationships in the world, wider body and within the gathering?'

Context can influence how quickly or slowly a new church bears fruit. Planting churches in chaotic contexts,[6] places where church attendance is virtually non-existent or where there is high deprivation can slow down fruit production. More time may be needed to adapt our methods to the context and it may require much more investment in relationships to cultivate ownership and belonging before we see people come to faith. Those in authority need to exercise patience and point pioneers towards supportive people who can help them find a way through the maze they may feel stuck in. Yet often when the key to the context is found and the door unlocked, it can reap a harvest later on. Sorted 1 had all these challenges in abundance; it took what seemed an eternity to break through and yet the harvest was well worth waiting for!

There are many times I felt a failure because our young people didn't match up to the expectations of one or two local Christian ministers. Our young people were expected to start car-washing, litter-picking and so on, alongside other Christians from local churches. It took me a long time to fully understand what was going on under the surface here. We began Sorted because there was a culture chasm between local churches and the culture of young people in most of Bradford. It was totally unrealistic and unfair to expect that once they became Christians, they would want to join older churchgoers in such activities!

It took a long time for Sorted young people to bear the fruit of growing in relationship with other churches. It began when we started looking for things that would work for our young people, not trying to meet local church expectations – meeting other young Christians at Soul Survivor worked, getting our bishop to come and baptize at Sorted worked, as did taking two or three young people regularly to visit local churches and briefly tell their story.

I soon figured out that it is better to gain little victories in this area, give young people the incentive to try other things in the future, build on the positives rather than coerce them into doing things that would only push them further away from other churches and make it harder to bear this fruit in the future.

This taught me a big lesson – fruitfulness doesn't look the same to everyone! People need to be careful when judging a church's fruitfulness against the yardstick of their own experience. It's better to ask, What is God doing among these people and how can I work to aid the process? For me, it was to stop listening to wrong expectations, see how God was working in young lives, and encourage them to share their experiences in local churches and so on.

Growth should be viewed as a spectrum where the direction of travel is more important than your position on the spectrum. Some Christians may expect your new people to get to level six because they themselves started at five, came to faith and moved on to six then seven. But the new people may come from a background of no Christian experience, so they begin at stage two and are now at three or four. Stage six can come later; it's the direction of travel that is important.

2 Flow

Although becoming fruitful in some areas can take patience and time, we should keep looking to the future, asking God to help us bear fruit in unfruitful areas. Having good connections and creating a flow from Sorted to other churches has been a slow process. However, in recent years we've built many connections between Sorted and other local churches. As our young people have supported local churches by serving the homeless, helping in holiday clubs and children's groups, speaking at events and fixing several church PA systems, their wider church horizon has broadened and their future options for church have expanded.

With 'flow', context matters – new people with previous church involvement are likely to find it easier to connect to others in local churches and therefore the 'flow' will come easier. New people of a fresh expression may need to search further afield to find other Christians of similar age or culture for an effective flow to happen, at least in the first few years. Genuine love can build bridges across the age or culture gap, but most people tend to swim in a sea they understand, so love has to lead to mutual understanding and a relationship of trust if it's to last.

3 Family

Plugging into wider networks can be a great way for new church members to grow in their faith. You may have to look around to find suitable resources for them to plug into. We've used resources from Soul Survivor and *Youthwork* magazine but we've adapted it to make it more relevant to our young people.

4 *Freedom*

Moynagh suggests that smaller contextual churches might need to find the appropriate amount of freedom that suits their stage of development. Some will be ready to self-govern. Others will need more outside help and support. This raises another question – let's suppose a new church grows quite a lot and has several different groups, how much freedom should each group be given?

Values can act as glue, holding the groups of a larger new church together. Each group should input into the discussion of what our values are. An agreed set of values should be sought. Values can act as the hard shoulder and central reservation[7] on a motorway. As an individual group travel down the motorway, they have freedom to move between lanes, change speed and even choose what vehicle to travel in, but the hard shoulder and central reservation provide helpful boundaries to drive within. Values become rules of the road so that the group has freedom within helpful guidelines.

A larger new church may define its values together. It might meet together for worship and teaching, providing depth and a bigger family identity. Individually, each smaller group may plan its own vision, decide how to spend its own finances, run its own group/s, while contributing to the larger church and remaining accountable.

MAKING IT SUSTAINABLE – PART 2

Moynagh shows how sustainability of a fresh expression can be evaluated by examining growth in the four sets of relationships that are at the heart of church and centred on Jesus:[8]

UP: relationships with the Father, Son and Spirit
OUT: relationships with the world

IN: relationships within the fellowship
OF: relationships with the wider Christian family. You are part of the Body of Christ.

The aim is for church members to grow in these four sets of relationships. The more people that are growing in these relationships, the more sustainable your fresh expression is likely to be.

Be specific

Perhaps at the start of the year, your team will prayerfully imagine what growth might look like in each of these four sets of relationships. You will want to keep it simple and concrete so every time a suggestion is made, ask yourselves, 'How will we recognize this?' So instead of saying, 'We would like people to grow in their discipleship', which can be too vague, ask, 'In what two or three ways would we like to see growth in discipleship?' Being specific helps us to picture the steps needed to be put in place to make it happen.

Evaluation will be the process of looking back, recognizing the fruit you've prayed for, recognizing the absence of certain fruit and/or the presence fruit you didn't expect.

Recently, we did a training session on 'being able to talk about your faith in God' because we recognized that when people are able to say a few words of testimony or witness to who God is in their lives, this helps them to verbalize what is internal and can lead to increased understanding and ownership of their faith. It also encourages others to speak about their faith and can be the beginning of a process where some may become evangelists, pastors or teachers. This specific focus on 'speaking about our faith' was one part of our desire to see people develop deeper discipleship. The specific actions needed to make it happen included a training session (including learning and role modelling speaking about faith), mini interviews (opportunities to speak about faith simply) and creating opportunities for people to lead discussion groups (to answer questions about their faith and develop cognitive learning). All three actions contribute in different ways to helping people speak about their faith.

Evaluating

After a few months, the team might evaluate the different specifics (e.g. speaking about faith) they've tried to grow in the four sets of relationships. Did they all happen? What were the results? What gaps remain in the life of the fresh expression? What is the Holy Spirit saying through all this? In the light of this prayerful discussion, what might growth in these relationships look like over the next few months? For example:

- Should we pay more attention to spiritual gifts?
- Should we encourage the community to support a project in the Global South?
- Should we be more proactive in inviting cafe guests to initiate or help with social events?
- Should the team attend a particular conference that our denomination or network is organizing?

You might want use the questions below to help evaluate growth in the four relationships. Comparing your answers to previous years' answers may reveal whether relationships are growing, staying the same or declining.

UP relationship

- What is the average attendance at our worship events?
- How many people attend Christian discovery groups and/or Christian formation or accountability groups?
- How many people are on a journey with God? How many Christians?
- How many people give financially on a regular basis?
- How many are involved in the community's mission activities?

OUT relationship

- How many people are served by the fresh expression each week?
- How many people does the fresh expression make contact with each week?
- Ask those in the community what impressions of the fresh expression they are getting.
- How many people are from another church? Once churched? Never churched?

OF relationship

- How many of the fresh expression's leaders and members attended events in the wider local church last year?
- How did the leaders and members contribute to the wider church last year?
- What proportion of the fresh expression's budget is spent on supporting Christians in the wider church?

IN relationship

- How many people attend the fresh expression regularly and identify with it?
- What proportion of the list attend weekly, monthly, quarterly?
- What proportion serves within the fresh expression?
- How many people are on the discipleship journey in one form or another?

Putting these questions into practice through a survey will give you definitive data. My experience is that you always learn new things about your fresh expression through asking people a set of questions – don't assume you already know the answers; doing the survey nearly always messes up assumptions! If your denomination or church network is looking to measure your progress, then this survey will provide some figures.

You can bring your results before the Lord in prayer, and then discuss with your team what specific actions you want to implement over the next few months.

Grace – by Steve Collins[9]

Here is an excerpt of the 20-year history of Grace, an alternative worship community based at St Mary's Church, Ealing – a lesson in sustainability.

'Our 10th anniversary in 2003 came as a bit of a shock, because we'd always thought of ourselves as fragile in the face of circumstances and liable to end at any moment; we had to readjust our mindset when we realized that we were in it for the long haul! Our 20th anniversary offers us opportunity for reflection and re-evaluation . . .

Grace is a strong example of what the Church Army's Research Unit recent report into Fresh Expressions of church and church plants calls 'lay-lay spare-time' leadership – people who are mostly not ordained and who do not have any formal training or accreditation. They generally serve in their spare time and so face all the associated limitations of resources and energy . . .

Over the last few years, individuals have faced major stage-of-life issues which make it hard to find the time and energy for Grace. Ironically, our deepening personal commitments to mission have also had an impact. With core members struggling to be available, or unwilling to commit, and a decline in the congregational numbers (probably for similar reasons), the structures we set up 10 years ago are proving hard to sustain. Our 19th year found us at a low ebb, barely able to make the monthly services happen. We openly discussed the possibility of giving up.

In the circumstances it didn't seem right to make a big fuss over our 20th anniversary. We had a fairly low-key celebration for the actual anniversary, and filled the rest of our 20th year by revisiting favourite services from the archives. The intention was to take them 'ready-made' to make things easy, but our creative instincts seem to have revived and most of the services so far have been significantly reinvented. It seems to be part of the DNA of Grace – even through all the changes in personnel over the years – that we have to reinvent things, we can't bear to do the same thing twice, even when it costs us or risks failure . . .

All of our structures are self-imposed, so the questions as we look forward are: What do we want to do now? What are we capable of doing now? What do we need to do, to continue as a missional and worshipping community?

For Grace the secret of longevity seems to be in having a mix of new people but also people who have been there for most or all of the community's life. The former stop it growing stale, repetitive or inward-looking, the latter carry the historical memory of the community, the wisdom and fortitude that comes from having been there and done that before. Don't have the new people, and you settle into a routine that offers nothing new for others or yourselves. Don't have the long-term people and you fight your first battles over and over again and never get past the beginners' stages.

For those just starting on this path, we offer two lessons from our experience: persistence, and publicity. Persistence is essential if you are to last long enough to grow into community and to develop your own mission. It turns failures into experience and success into a foundation. Publicity brings outsiders to inspire you and stop you becoming a clique. It allows you to share your wisdom and receive wisdom from others. It lets you be part of a bigger picture.

How long will Grace last? One of the ways that Grace is sustainable is by having group leadership that doesn't need to transition from one leader to another. In a sense we're always in transition as people take up and step away responsibility, but it's balanced by having a mix of new and long-term people in the centre, as described. The founder of Grace is still a member, but he doesn't have to be a 'leader' unless he feels like it!'

Notes

1 Michael Moynagh, *Church for Every Context*, London: SCM Press, 2012, p. 411.
2 Some people worry that mentoring your successor doesn't give them enough freedom to be themselves, 'Just let them get on with it, as happens with a new vicar!' Yet a new church losing its founder is usually much more fragile than an established church that may have seen several changes of leadership over the decades, so this transition needs much more careful handling. Mentoring your successor is about giving the new leader a solid foundation to start from; it's about removing as many blind spots as possible so that the transition is as smooth as possible. A good leader going in blind, making mistakes or changing things too quickly in an established church can have devastating consequences, such as losing 20–30% of the congregation. In a new church with only one previous leader, similar mistakes could lead to closure! A recent fresh expression of church declined from thirty to three people when the leader left because the succession planning had been based on the Anglican interregnum model where a vicar leaves and six months later the next vicar arrives. It was much too early in the life of this new and fragile church to be left leaderless for six months.
3 Idea developed by Henry Venn: www.acpi.org.uk/stories/3 3 Self.htm.
4 Moynagh, *Church for Every Context*, pp. 405–7.
5 Church Army, *Encounters on the Edge*, issue 4, 'Eternity', p. 20.
6 Moynagh, *Church for Every Context*, p. 199.
7 Taken from a talk by John Mumford at a Vineyard conference, 2003.
8 Michael Moynagh, *Being Church, Doing Life: Creating Gospel Communities where Life Happens*, Oxford: Monarch, 2014, pp. 338–42.
9 Story by Steve Collins: www.freshexpressions.org.uk/stories/grace.

Bibliography

Bing, Alan, http://churcharmy.org.uk/Publisher/File.aspx?ID=138623.

Breen, Mike, *Outside In*, London: Scripture Union, 1993.

CPAS Arrow Leadership Course, https://www.cpas.org.uk.

Cray, Graham (ed.), *Mission-Shaped Church*, London: Church House Publishing, 2004.

Cray, Graham, *Making Disciples in Fresh Expressions of Church*, Bozeat: Fresh Expressions, 2013.

Croft, Steven, Dalpra, Claire and Lings, George, *Starting a Fresh Expression*, Bozeat: Fresh Expressions, 2006.

Donovan, Vincent, *Christianity Rediscovered*, London: SCM Press, 1978.

Fresh Expression UK Share booklets, www.freshexpressions.org.uk/share /booklets.

Frost, Michael and Hirsch, Alan, *The Shape of Things to Come: Innovation and Mission for the 21st-Century Church*, Peabody, MA: Hendrickson, 2003.

Fung, Raymond, *The Isaiah Vision: An Ecumenical Strategy for Congregational Evangelism*, Geneva: World Council of Churches, 1992.

Lings, George, *Encounters on the Edge*, http://www.encountersontheedge .org.uk.

Mallon, Paddy, *Calling a City Back to God*, Eastbourne: Kingsway, 2003.

Moynagh, Michael, *Church for Every Context*, London: SCM Press, 2012.

Moynagh, Michael, *Being Church, Doing Life: Creating Gospel Communities where Life Happens*, Oxford: Monarch, 2014.

Moynagh, Michael and Freeman, Andy, *How Can Fresh Expressions Emerge?* Bozeat: Fresh Expressions, 2011.

Potter, Phil, *The Challenge of Cell Church: Getting to Grips with Cell Church Values*, Abingdon: BRF/CPAS, 2001.

Pytches, David, *Come Holy Spirit: Learning How to Minister in Power*, London: Hodder & Stoughton, 1985.

Ridley-Duff, Rory and Bull, Mike, *Understanding Social Enterprise: Theory and Practice*, London: Sage, 2011.

Stepping into Evangelism booklet, http://www.churcharmy.org.uk/Groups
    /244431/Church_Army/Church_Army/Resources/Stepping_into
    _evangelism/Stepping_into_evangelism.aspx.
Vineyard UK, *Cutting Edge Magazine*.
Warren, Rick, *The Purpose Driven Church*, Grand Rapids, Michigan:
    Zondervan, 1995.
Youth Bible, New Century Version, Nashville, TN: Thomas Nelson,
    2010.

Websites

www.acpi.org.uk/stories/33 Self.htm
www.biblegateway.com
www.freshexpressions.org.uk
www.goodreads.com
www.oxforddictionaries.com
www.soulsurvivor.com
www.truefreedomtrust.co.uk

Index of Names and Subjects

Index of Bible References